Contents

IT USER FUNDAMENTALS

Introduction to IT, File management, Web browsing, Email

Learning outcomes

After completing this lesson, students will be able to:
   a. describe IT, its components, types, and legal requirements;
   b. manage data, files, and folders.
   c. organise files by creating folders, directories, and subfolders.
   d. create, save files in directories or folders, and retrieve files.
   e. make backup copies of your files, find, copy, rename, and delete files.
   f. utilise a web browser effectively, use a search engine, and print web results.
   g. operate an email client efficiently, construct emails, and correctly employ email elements like "To:," "Cc:," "Subject:," and attach files.
   h. use accurate text-processing techniques, SPaG, and proofreading.

Introduction: Basic Information Technology (IT) Concepts

Information technology (IT) is the improved use of automated tools and systems in daily life and business to complete daily tasks, including making decisions. The impact of IT may be seen in many fields, including business, manufacturing, industry, aviation, medicine, and education, to name a few. The work and efforts that humans once performed manually are now done so with technology and at verifiable efficiencies. The phrase "information technology" refers to the evolution and advances in communication, quality, speed, capacity, availability, integrity, and security on the outputs that were made possible by IT.

Types of IT Systems

Computers, communication networks, and security are three categories of IT systems tools that each consist of hardware, software, firmware, and manware.

Computer System –

A computer is an electronic device that stores and processes data in accordance with predetermined rules to provide the intended result. The four (4) main peripherals or devices that make up a computer system are known as input devices (such as a keyboard and mouse) for accepting data into the system; processing devices (such as the base unit's processors) for processing and calculating data; backing storage devices (such as the primary store (known as Random Access Memory (RAM)), secondary store (known as internal hard disks and auxiliary store (memory stick, external hard disk)) for storing data during processing and/or retrieving stored data for processing and finally, the output devices, such as printers and Visual Display Units (VDU), for disseminating processed data. Softcopy refers to information displayed on a computer VDU screen, whereas hardcopy refers to information printed directly onto paper. Below is a block diagram typical of a computer system showing the data flow direction (arrow heads):

Introduction

The intent of this book is to provide you with a thorough grasp of the methods and processes employed in computer applications software for the processing of data and information in business, organisations, and related fields. The common integrated software programme that is utilised throughout the book for all documentation is Microsoft Office. You will be directed through the critical steps of the process and applications of spreadsheet, presentation, database, and mail merge apps whether you are a student in a university, college, or commercial training programme. This will help you perform your work more successfully.

You don't need to have much prior knowledge, and there is no attempt to teach you everything; nonetheless, the information is comprehensive and in-depth enough so that you might succeed in any job.

This goal of this section is to introduce the context of the book, give you a sense of its substance, and explain how to navigate your way around.

The ICT Functional Skills Level 2 book is designed to help learners build a strong foundation in using Information and Communication Technology (ICT) for work and personal use. This book is divided into 7 easy tutorial lessons, covering the fundamentals of ICT, Excel Spreadsheet, Spreadsheet IF Functions, PowerPoint Presentation, Access Database, and Word Mail Merge.

In the first lesson, learners will be introduced to the basic concepts of ICT, including hardware, software, and file management. The second lesson will focus on Excel Spreadsheet, where learners will learn how to create and format spreadsheets, perform calculations, and use basic functions. In the third and fifth lessons, learners will explore advanced spreadsheet functions such as IF functions.

The fourth lesson will introduce learners to PowerPoint Presentation, where they will learn how to create professional presentations, add multimedia, and use animations and transitions. The sixth lesson will focus on Access Database, where learners will learn how to design, create, query databases as well as generate forms and reports.

In the seventh lesson, learners will be introduced to Word Mail Merge, where they will learn how to create letters, and merging fields for labels, and envelopes using data from a notepad, spreadsheet or database. Finally, each of the seven lessons are scenario-based and would support learners to apply all the skills they have learned throughout the book and put them into practice when completing a comprehensive project such as the ICT functional skills exams.

This book is written in simple language, and the tutorials are supported by clear instructions, screenshots, and practice exercises to help learners reinforce their understanding of the concepts. By the end of this book, learners will have a strong foundation in the core ICT skills needed for today's workplace.

Background

The methodology employed in this book is condensed and founded on widely established theory and practise of computer applications at levels 1 and 2. As a result, you won't need to master the intricate details of spreadsheet models, database design, or normalisation procedures. You are free to use more imagination as you learn because these subtleties are not covered in this text.

Acknowledgement

I would like to acknowledge, thank, and express my gratitude to a number of educational stakeholders, including the City & Guilds awarding body, whose exam sample papers were used in parts of this book, my teaching colleagues, whose input during staff meetings and standardisation meetings may have influenced the book's outcome, and most importantly, my numerous students across the globe, whose participation in my lessons may also have influenced my teaching style and efficacy.

Dedication

For Patsy, my wife, and our children, who are all grown and independent.

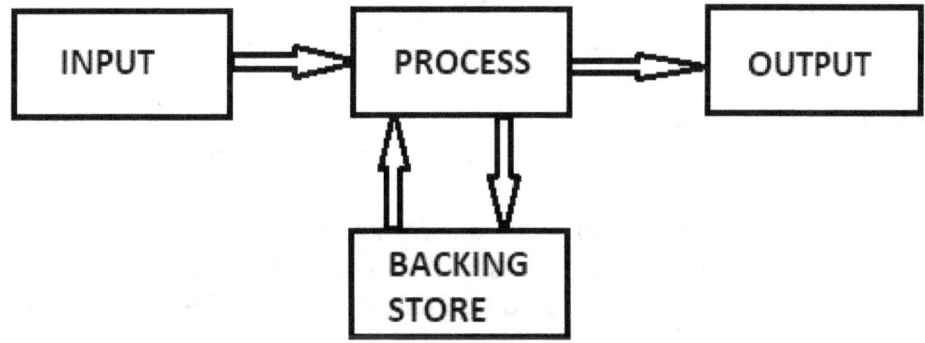

Block diagram of a Computer System

Communication Networks –

A communication network is a grouping of two or more computers that allows them to communicate, share files and folders, and/or exchange data and information. Network systems are the general name for the connecting (or channeling) of these machines. The topology of computer networks, which determines how they are connected, can take many different forms. The Bus topology, Star topology, Ring topology, and Mesh topology are the four most popular network topologies. The Internet is a prime example of a computer network because it made it possible for people, corporations, and everything else to be connected online today. We have the "C" in IT, i.e., information communication technology, because of the Internet's development and realisation of its potential.

Types of Network Topology

Below are infographics depicting the four typical network topologies or layouts:

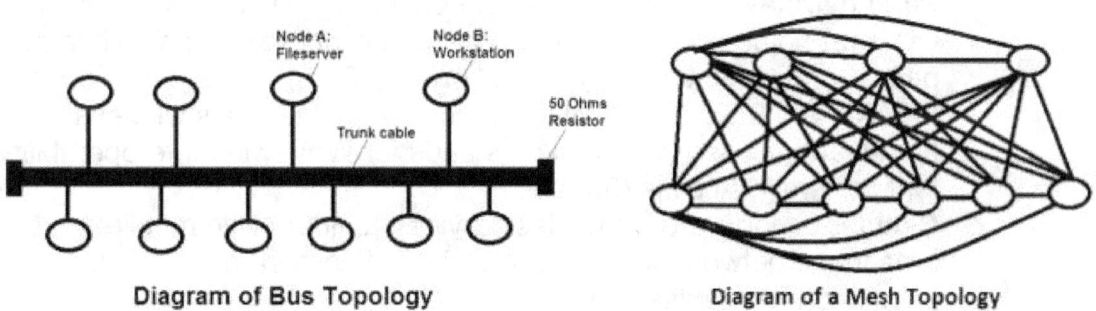

Diagram of Bus Topology

Diagram of a Mesh Topology

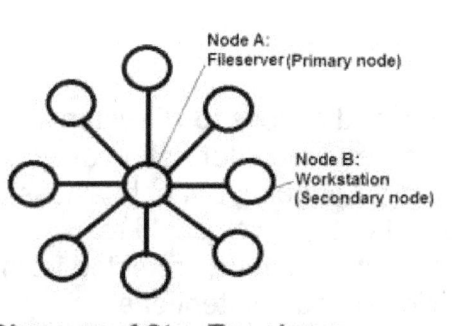

Diagram of Star Topology

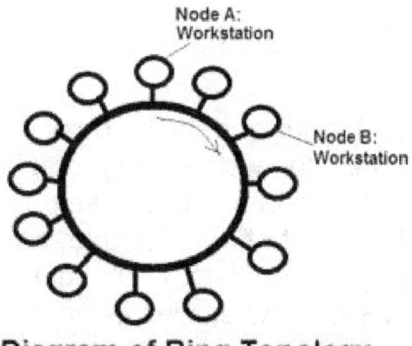

Diagram of Ring Topology

Types of Communication Networks
Communication networks typically come in the following forms:

- **Local Area Network (LAN)** - This term refers to the network connectivity within a single geographic area, such as a college campus, a house, building or location.
- **Wide Area Network (WAN),** also known as Long Haul Network, is the network connectivity that connects LAN over and beyond various geographical locations, such as a network connection between two or more campuses or sites of a college.
- The network connectivity that connects multiple LANs (such as workplace LANs) in a small metro area is known as a **Metropolitan Area Network (MAN)**. In a City Center or Downtown, a collection of businesses next to one another may feel the need to connect their LANs.
- **Personal Area Network (PAN)** is the short-ranged network connectivity we have with Bluetooth, infrared, and airdrop for sending and exchanging data, information, and files over our smartphones, iPads, and other portable digital devices.
- **Wireless Technologies** - Broad categories of wireless networks include:
  - **Wireless personal-area network (WPAN):** only works within a few feet of the user (Bluetooth).
  - **Wireless LAN (WLAN)** - Operates within a few hundred feet of the device.
  - **Wireless wide-area network (WWAN)** - Operates over kilometres of space.
  - **Bluetooth,** an IEEE 802.15 WPAN technology that allows devices to pair with one another and communicate at distances of up to 0.05 miles (100m).
  - **Wi-Fi (wireless fidelity),** an IEEE 802.11 WLAN standard, allows users (at home and at work) to access networks and transmit data, phone, and video up to 0.18 miles away (300m).
  - **WiMAX**, an IEEE 802.16 WWAN technology that uses wireless broadband access up to 30 km, stands for Worldwide Interoperability for Microwave Access (50 km).
  - **Cellular broadband** - provides service providers with mobile broadband network access for a variety of corporate, national, and international organisations.
  - **Satellite Broadband** - gives remote locations network connectivity using a directed satellite dish.

IT Security
IT security is the barrier or defense against unauthorised access to IT systems, including computers, as well as the protection of the data and information used or stored within. Without data, a business runs the danger of going out of business or having to shell out a lot of cash to rekey all of the lost data, which could result in lost clients and compromised data. Digital data and computers can be protected from internal and external risks as well as hostile (malicious) and unintentional (accidental) threats.

Strong passwords, two-factor authentication, regular data backups, data encryption, the use of biometrics, protection from power fluctuations, and the use of software protection to "lock" particular files on a disc so that they are read-only and cannot be overwritten are defenses against these threats.

Companies maintain IT security by employing security rules and security tools like firewalls, demilitarised zones (DMZ), antivirus, and antimalware software to recognise, halt, and mitigate threats. Adequate staff training is an undervalued requirement for safety and security in any IT system implementations.

IT Systems Components
The four primary elements of IT systems are as follows (I refer to them as the "4-wares"):
- **Hardware** – refers to the visible and tangible components of a computer system, such as the keyboard, mouse, VDU, cables, base unit, printer, memory stick, etc.
- **Software** - The intangible, unobservable components of a computer system that include the operating system, data stored on a memory stick, and programme containing instructions. Software is only imagined or conceived.
- **Firmware** - is a piece of software or a short set of instructions that is etched into the Read Only Memory (ROM) chip of your computer system to turn it on when it is switched on. Additionally, it starts the bootstrap process for the Basic Input-Output System (BIOS).
- **Manware** – is the human computer operator; without a human computer operator, a computer or IT tool would just be a piece of equipment. An operator is a crucial component of an IT system, and as such, they must be acknowledged and recognised.

IT Legislation
Using technology has emancipated information and made it available to everyone; yet, unintended consequences may not have been foreseen. The ability to access, utilise, and/or control new technology must be regulated by laws that consider this innovation.
- With the development and application of new technologies, new issues and conflicts have emerged, including those related to ergonomics, safety, and health. - the careful and secure use of IT
- Intellectual property issues: Can a computer programme or set of data be stolen?
- Important facts: Who should have access to personal information kept on computers? Who ought to be able to access, use, or save data?
- Concerns about data privacy.

The aforementioned issues sparked the following judicial and legislative responses:
- The 1974 Act on Health and Safety at Work (occupational laws, principles and design that are intended to keep people safe from injury or disease at the workplace)
- In 2018, the General Data Protection Regulation (GDPR) took the place of the Data Protection Act (DPA) and Directive 95/46/EC.

- With the UK's departure from the EU in 2021, the GDPR has changed back to the DPA.
- The 1988 Act on Copyright, Design, and Patents (law protecting the rights of owner of intellectual property such as inventions, literatures, books, art, music, literary works like computer programme, etc.)
- The Computer Misuse Act of 1990 (law prohibiting unauthorised access to, use of, and tampering with of, an organization's personal data and computer materials).

File Management

File management and data handling are the processes used by computer users to create an effective filing system on their computer's hard drive, memory stick, and/or cloud storage solution with relevant names given to all documents. Making files, subfolders, and folders/directories organised for efficient data location, file retrieval, and backup is part of the procedure.

The ability to save files (such as spreadsheets) in directories and folders as well as other directories and folders is a basic requirement for computer maintenance. Users must also be able to backup their data, locate and recover data from other discs and places (folders and subfolders), rename data, and delete data and folders that are no longer required.

One of the functional abilities examined in ICT exams is effective file management, which involves making folders and subfolders and storing newly created files inside of them:

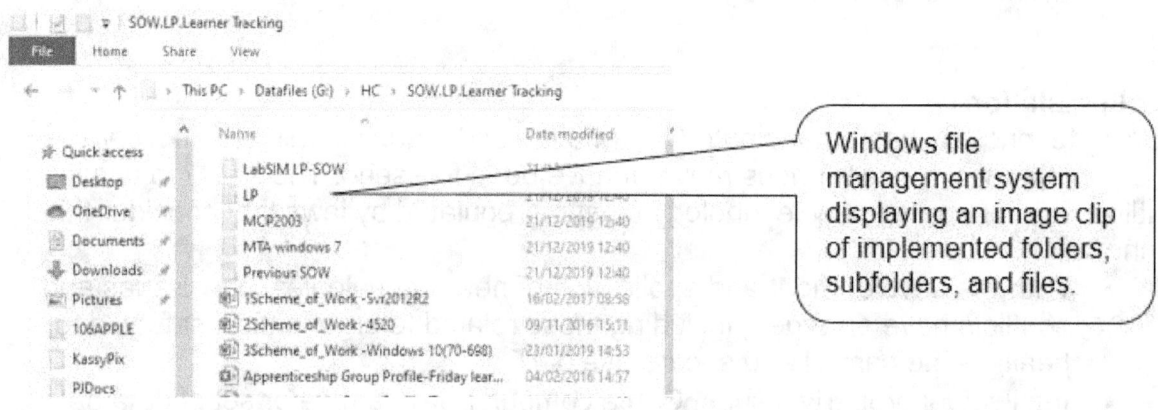

Windows file management system displaying an image clip of implemented folders, subfolders, and files.

Attention: All file management results and the aforementioned image(s) must be copied and then pasted into your Word document as evidence.

Web Browsing

A web browser is a piece of software used to access and read web pages on the internet, the World Wide Web, and other internet objects, including search engines. WorldWideWeb (www), which later went by the name Nexus, was the first web browser created by Sir Tim Berners-Lee and released in 1990.

Due to technology improvements, the early web browser underwent tremendous modification to become the well-known web browsers of today, such as Microsoft Edge, Google Chrome, Mozilla Firefox, Apple Safari, and Opera.

The bulk of internet users nowadays would have used a web browser on their PCs or mobile devices to access the internet and see websites like Facebook, Twitter, Instagram, and YouTube. To look for specific bits of information, they would have also used online search engines like google.com.

As part of the broad framework for the functional skill in ICT, a student will need to do a search for the provided information. Also, they must copy and paste the words they entered in the search engine's search bar and/or the search results into a Word document that they may use to respond to a particular query.

To pass the functional skills ICT exam, a candidate must show proficiency using a web browser to view a specific website or page, a search engine to locate information, copying and pasting that information, using it to respond to a question, and/or pasting the web address of that information into a Word document.

Typical Example
Culled: *from the Functional Skills ICT Level 2 Funfair Sample Exams Paper by City & Guilds of London:*

- *Utilising questions from Section A, search engine activity; using a web browser and the associated image clips*

   Search for 'Mercure Hythe imperial hotel'

- ***Below is the result of the Search string used for the 'Mercure Hythe Hotel':***

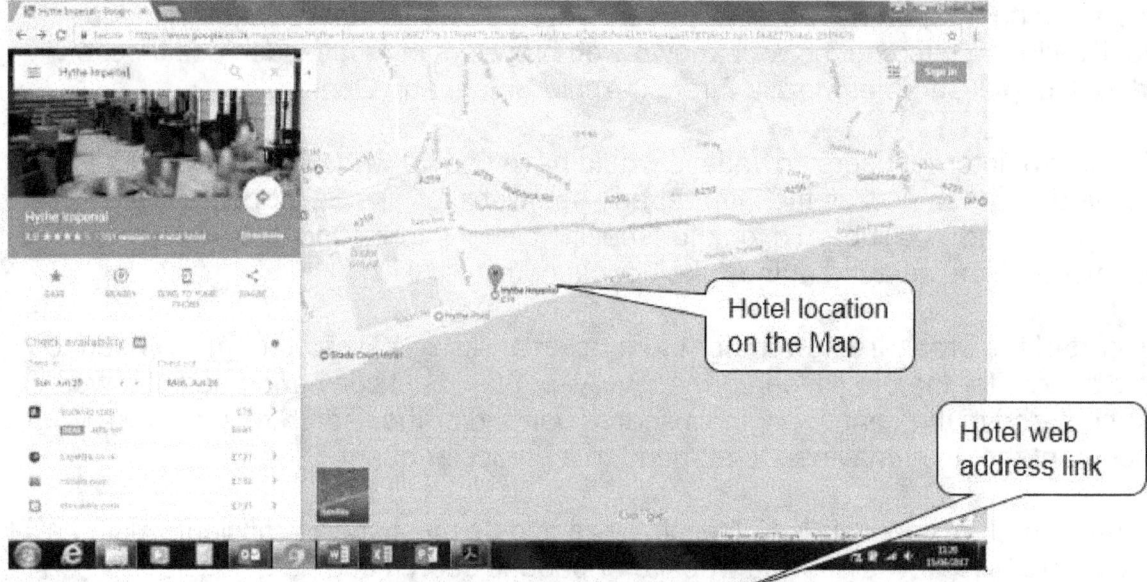

https://www.google.co.uk/maps/place/Hythe+Imperial/@51.0682776,1.0949475,15z/data=
!4m5!3m4!1s0x0:0xc419334c4aad5787!8m2!3d51.0682776!4d1.0949475

- **Bookmarked Restaurant Opening Times**

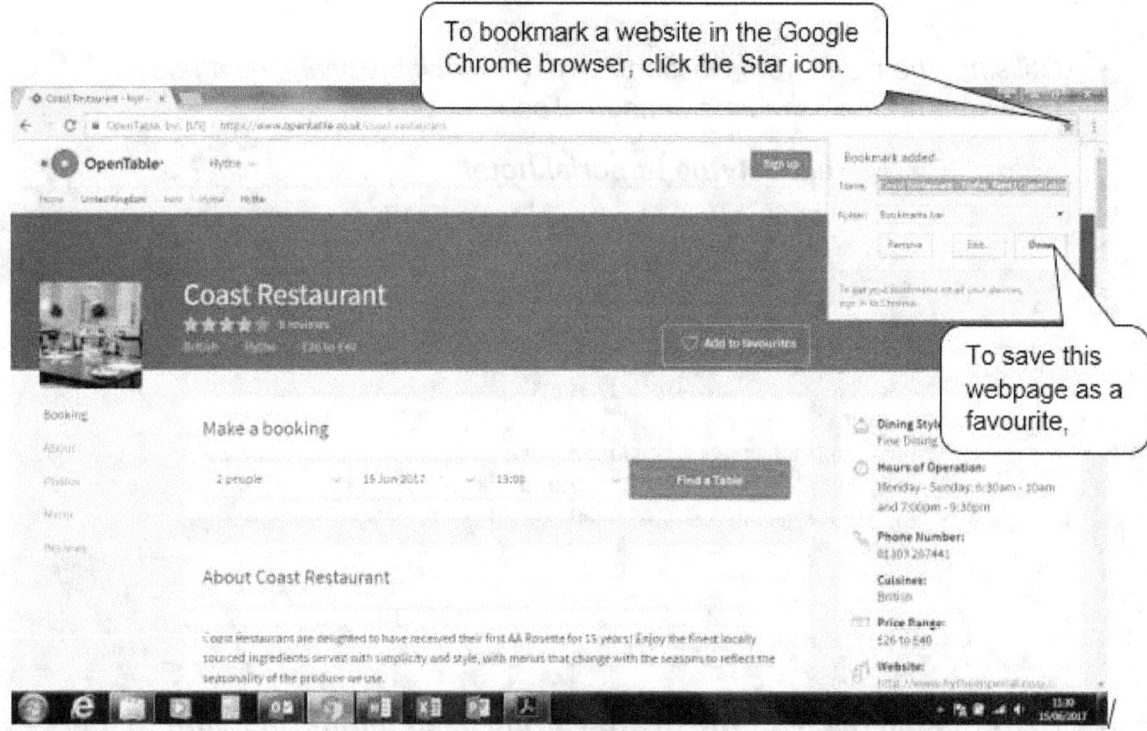

Reminder: You must copy all website results, including photos and links, as stated above, and paste them in your Word document as proof.

Email

Email is the term for electronic mail. It is an electronic message transmitted from one computer user to another via a communication network. Emails connected through external gateways, however, allow for global email delivery. Certain emails can only be sent through a certain network or computer system. Email has many advantages, including the ability to send messages to multiple recipients, send them quickly, and attach files.

A learner must demonstrate effective use of email and all of its elements, including "To," "From," "Subject," "Attachment," acceptable text body, opening greeting, closing/signature, and Utilize proper Spelling, Punctuation, and Grammar (SPaG), as follows:

- *Evidence of composed email to manager and attachment*

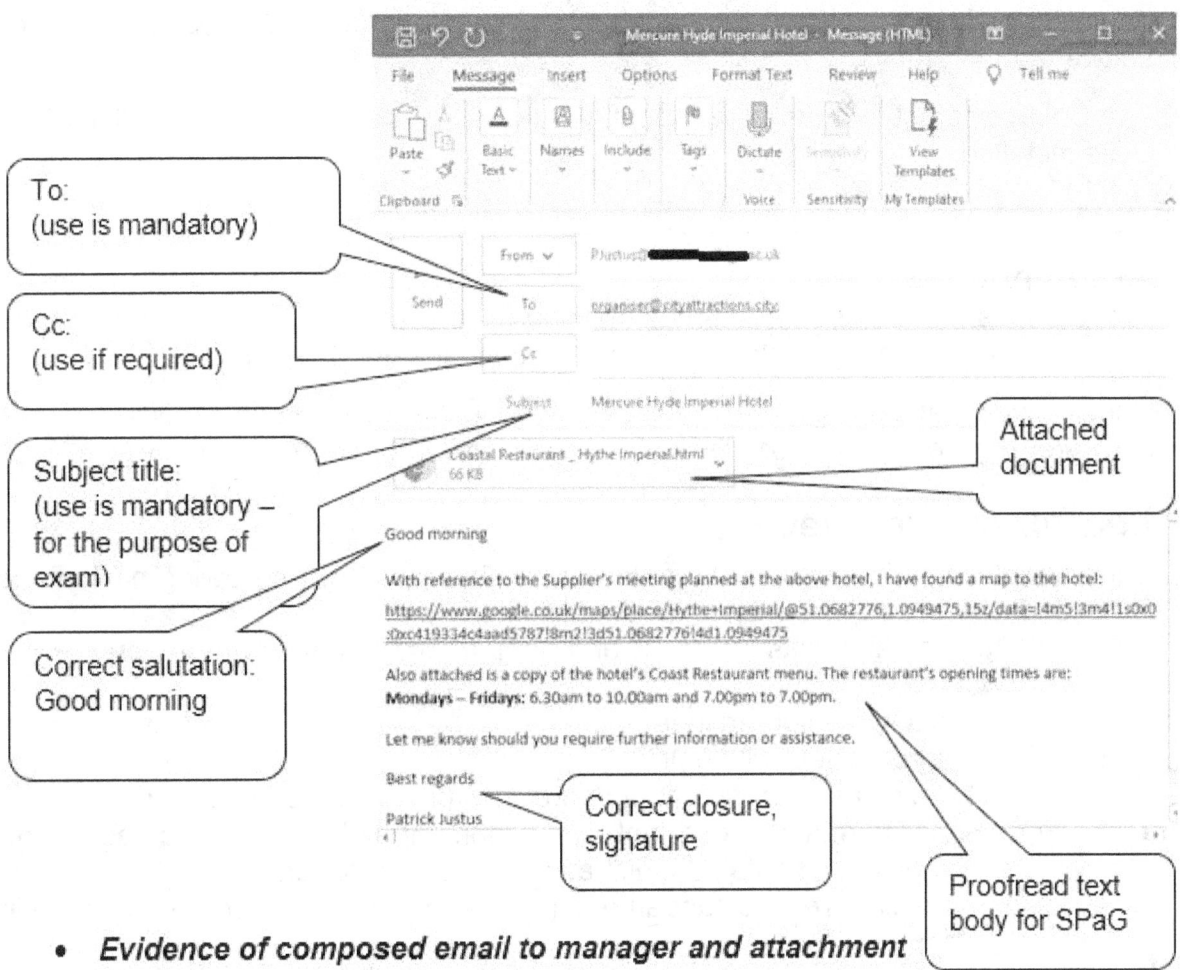

- *Evidence of composed email to manager and attachment*

Reminder: You might not have to send the email directly; instead, you'll have to copy it exactly as written above and paste it in your Word document as proof.

EXCEL SPREADSHEET APPLICATION SOFTWARE

SCENARIO

As a junior developer in a college, it is your responsibility to design and create a straightforward information system that can store student academic data and provide progress and performance reporting. The system that is put in place should be able to provide additional necessary reports as well as record students' marks and grades earned in various course modules and units. Respective kids receive their reports informing them of their accomplishments at their home addresses.

Your task is to create the design and build the system, demonstrating your proficiency with level 2 Word, Spreadsheets, Presentation, and Database application software.

The College computer runs on Microsoft Windows 10 and has Microsoft Office 365 Suite installed.

Assumption

This spreadsheet workbook assumes that you have some familiarity with the fundamentals of Microsoft Office, file organisation, and word processing.

Understanding and using Excel's window will benefit from any prior Windows software experience. The Excel window is very similar to the Word window.

Learning outcomes

After completing this session, students will be able to use the following basic Excel Spreadsheet features, commands, and functions:

    a. List the key elements, function, and menu-bar commands of the spreadsheet programme.
    b. Import data into a spreadsheet;
    c. Open a spreadsheet with data;
    d. Enter data; edit; printer setup; print preview; print layouts, print area;
    e. Formatting information: font, font size, alignment, bold, italics, and page layout
    f. Data modelling and data administration with emphasis on:
        i. formula use and fundamental operations (sum, average, count, min, max)
        ii. data structures, including "IF," "AND," "OR," and "Nested IF" functions
        iii. Present data in a formula view
        iv. Comparing relative and absolute cells (F4 key, naming cell)
    g. Manipulation of data
        v. Use extensive spreadsheets; divide worksheets, freeze page headers, and locate text and cells
        vi. Data validation, sorting, filtering, and graphing/charting

What is a Spreadsheet?

A spreadsheet is a programme composed of rows and columns laid out in grids. It is generally used to enter, edit, format, sort, and execute mathematical operations before being saved, retrieved, and printed. A cell is the point where a row and a column meet. Microsoft Excel is currently the most widely used spreadsheet application programme in the industry.

Worksheets are the name for Excel spreadsheets. Workbooks are collections of worksheets. There could be a lot of worksheets in a workbook file.

Types of information

The three major forms of data that can be entered into a spreadsheet cell are as follows:

- **Label** (text entries, left-aligned text, alphanumeric cell coordinates, or numerals as text with an apostrophe before the number, such as "2567")
- **Values** (numbers, numbers used in calculations, numbers aligned to the right, and ####, which denotes a column width insufficient to accommodate a number);
- **Formula** (number entered into a computation or formula; formulas begin with a "=" symbol; for example, C3+D3+E3 denotes the sum of the contents of cells C3, D3, and E3).

Arithmetic Operators

The arithmetic symbols below instruct the Excel spreadsheet to carry out mathematical operations:

Arithmetic Operator	Definition	Example of the definition	Meaning
+	Addition	=B3+C3	Add the values in B3 and C3 together.
-	Subtract	=F12-22	From the contents of cell F12, deduct 22.
*	Multiplication	=A3*B3	Multiply the value in cell A3 by the value in cell B3
/	Division	=C3/C6	Divide the contents of cell C3 by the contents of cell C6
^	Exponentiation	=C12^6	Raise the value in cell C12 to the sixth power

Excel Spreadsheet Cells

A **cell range** is a group of two or more cells that are close to one another. For instance, the range of cells E3:H3 represents the information in cells E3, F3, G3, and H3. For use in a computation or formula, for example, a group of cells can be given a specific name.

When employed in a formula, **cell referencing** stands in for the column letter and row number (for example, H2). If you modify the contents of a cell in a formula, the worksheet will immediately update it everywhere the cell is used in a calculation. This is done by using cell references in a formula to activate Excel's recalculation capability.

Types of Cell References

There are **three** primary categories of cell references:

- **Relative cell referencing** means that cells adjust to their new location when copied.
- **Absolute cell referencing** means that cells do not change when moved or copied to a new cell. To reference an absolute cell, use the $ sign. The $ symbol can be automatically added to a formula by using the F4 key.
- **Mixed cell referencing**, which includes references to both absolute and relative cells.

Functions

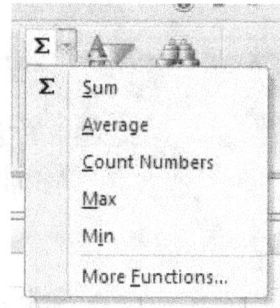

- A spreadsheet's built-in formulae are known as functions. Formulas and functions in a spreadsheet start with the equal sign ("=").

- AUTOSUM picklist arrow

- *fx* on the formulae bar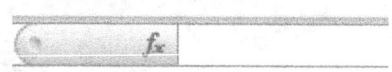

Example of a function:

  ◦ =AVERAGE(E6:E18)

  ◦ Use a range of cells (E6:E18)

  ◦ Colon means Excel will average the contents of cells E6 through E18

Common Formulas/Functions

Functions	Example of usage	Meaning
SUM	=SUM(E6:E18)	Calculates the sum of values in a range of cells, E6:E18
AVERAGE	=AVERAGE(E6:E18)	Calculates the average of values in a range of cells, E6:E18
COUNT	COUNT(E6:E18)	Calculates the number of values in a range of cells, E6:E18
MAX	=MAX(E6:E18)	Displays the largest value in a range of cells, E6:E18
MIN	=MIN(E6:E18)	Displays the smallest value in a range of cells, E6:E18
MEDIAN	=MEDIAN(E6:E18)	Displays the middle value in a range of cells, E6:E18
ROUND	=ROUND(E6,0)	Round content of cell E6 to zero
COUNT IF	=COUNTIF(E6:E18),1)	Count the number of 1s in the range of cells, E6:E18
IF	=IF(test_value, value_if_yes, value_if_no)	Value selection through argument testing(s)

Common shortcuts for spreadsheets

For quick spreadsheet manipulation, keyboard shortcuts are highly helpful. The following is a collection of some quick keyboard combinations or shortcuts for Excel spreadsheets:

- **F3** will Opens a dialog box to paste a Named Range into a formula.
- **F6** will Moves to the next pane in a split worksheet.
- **Ctrl | ;** will Inserts the current date.
- **Ctrl | 1** will Displays the Format Cells dialog box.
- **Ctrl | F3** will Opens the Define Name dialog box.
- **Ctrl | F6** will Moves to the next workbook window.
- **Shift | F3** will Inserts an equal sign (=) and opens the Paste Function dialog box to help you pick a formula.
- **Shift | F6** will Moves to the previous pane.
- **Shift | F10** will Displays the shortcut menu that applies to the selection.
- **Ctrl | Shift | A** will: Use this combination after typing a function name, and it will automatically enter the parentheses and the argument names for the function you typed.

- **Ctrl | Shift | F3** will Automatically create Named Ranges from the headers for the selected table of data with row or column headers.
- **Ctrl | Shift | F6** will Moves back to the last workbook window.
- **Ctrl | Shift | $** will Formats the current cells as Currency.
- **Ctrl | Shift | #** will Applies the Date format.
- **Alt | =** will Inserts the AutoSum function.
- **Alt | F8** will Displays the Macro dialog box.
- **Alt | F11** will Opens the VBA Editor or switches to it if it's already open.

Print Area

It's a good idea to use print Area when you simply need to print a small portion or area of a huge spreadsheet.

The following steps should be taken in Print Preview mode to set specific print areas:
a. Select the cells you want to print
b. On the menu bar, Select **Page Layout | Print Area**
c. Set Print Area
d. Click Print

To Clear the Print Area
a. On the menu bar, Select **Page Layout | Print Area**
b. Clear Print Area

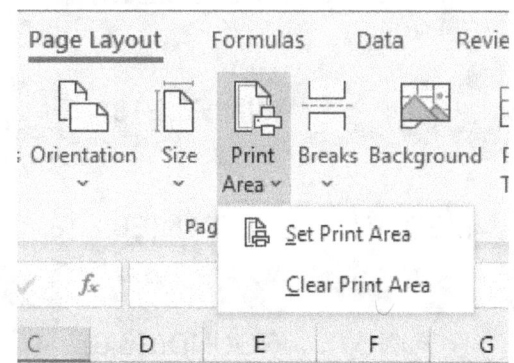

Freeze Titles

When dealing with a large spreadsheet, freeze titles are useful features since they allow you to scroll horizontally and/or vertically while still being able to see the column and/or row titles. You can choose one of three distinct views (freeze Panes, freeze Top Row, or freeze First Column) to use this feature, as seen in the image clip below, by selecting the **View** menu | **Freeze Panes** icon:

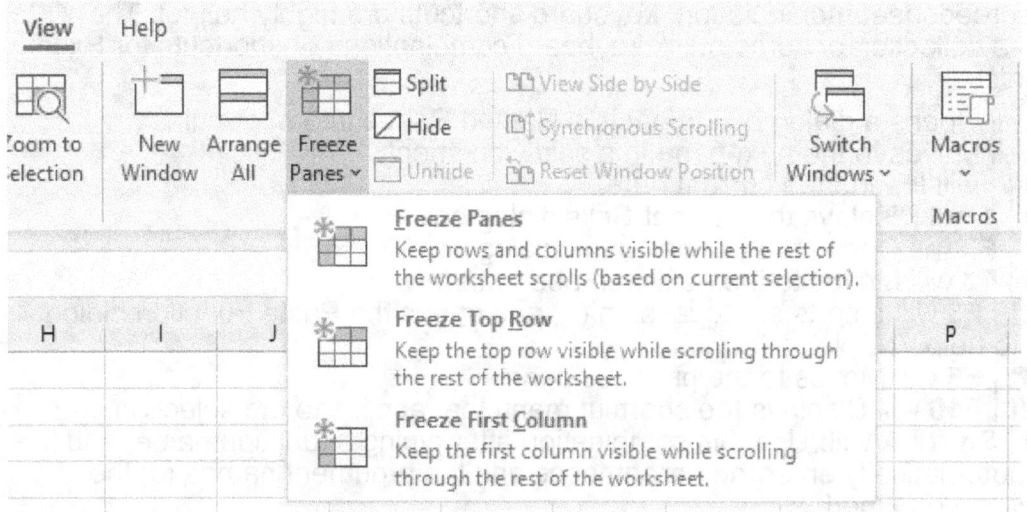

Spreadsheet Implementation and Modelling

Design and Develop a Students' Mark Sheet System

Step 1:
Launch the spreadsheet programme in the appropriate way (this example launches Microsoft Excel from Windows 10 and Office 2016).

On the Windows | Start-up interface, a part of Microsoft Windows 10 with a range of software icons is depicted in the image above. Locate the Microsoft Excel 2016 tile, click on it as shown below:

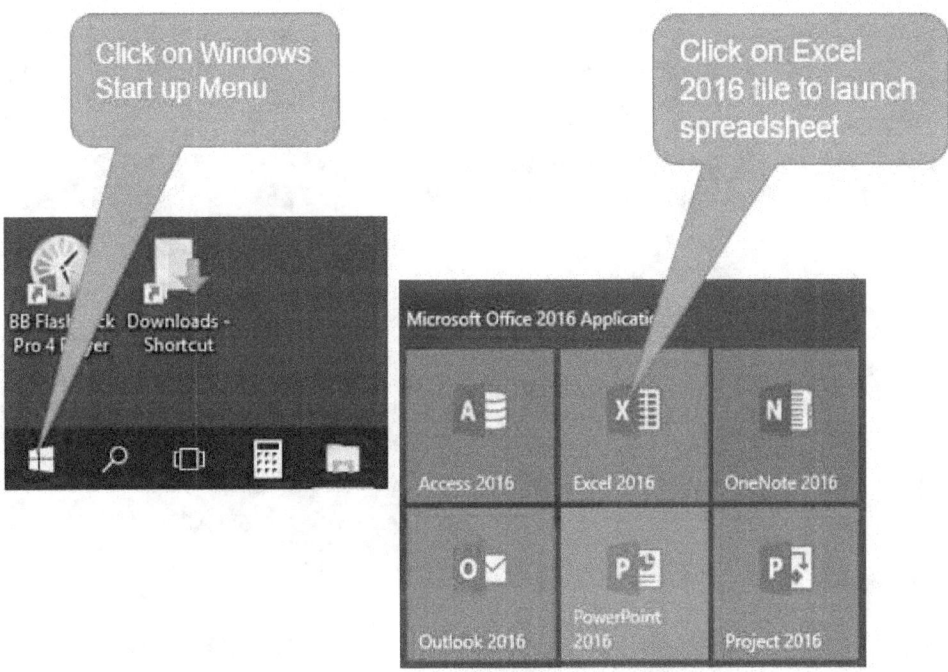

To start a new Workbook, then choose Blank Workbook from the pop-up menu that follows:

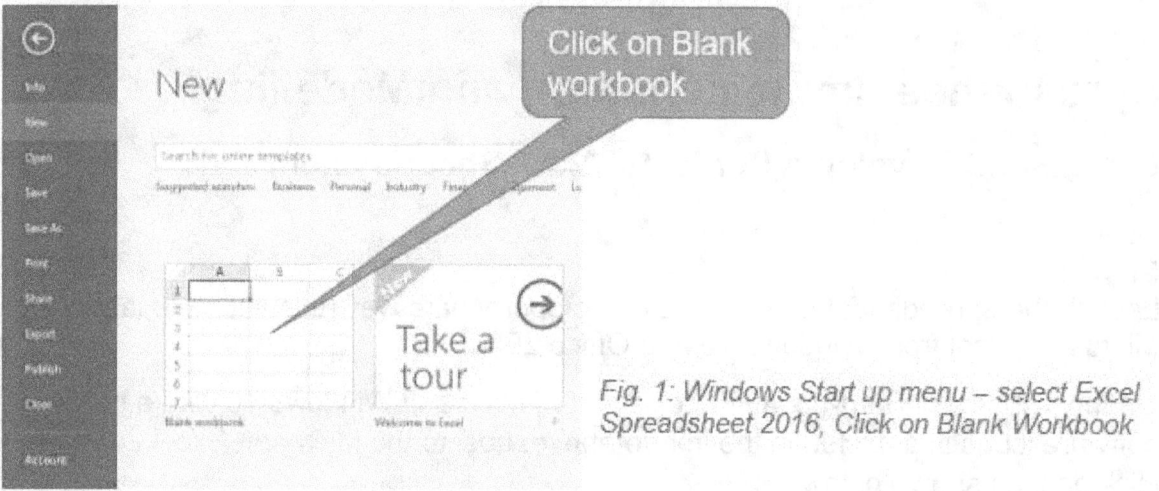

Fig. 1: Windows Start up menu – select Excel Spreadsheet 2016, Click on Blank Workbook

When launched correctly, the Excel Workbook will appear as follows:

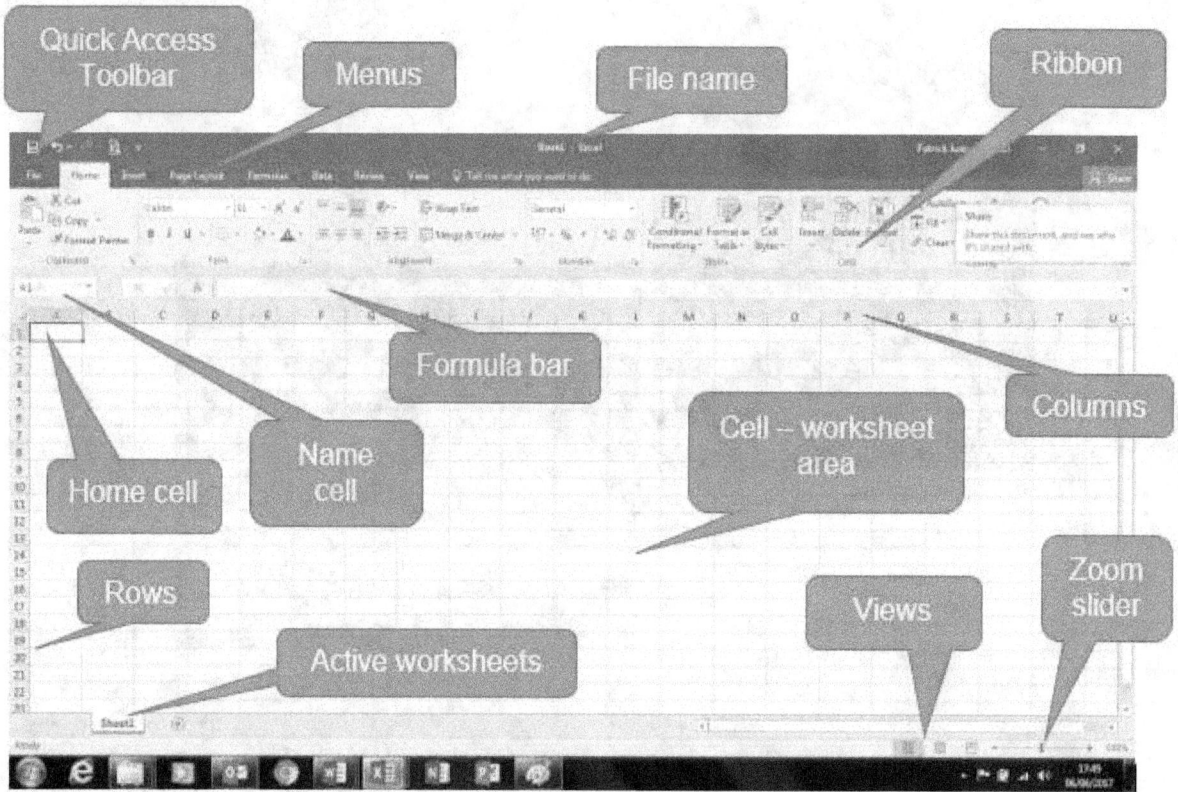

Fig. 2: The above diagram illustrates, identifies the common parts of Excel Spreadsheet workbook (a collection of spreadsheets is a workbook).

File menu tab – opens menus for information, new files, file opening and saving, printing, and a few additional utilities, such as Excel Options.

Quick Access Toolbar - icons from the picklist

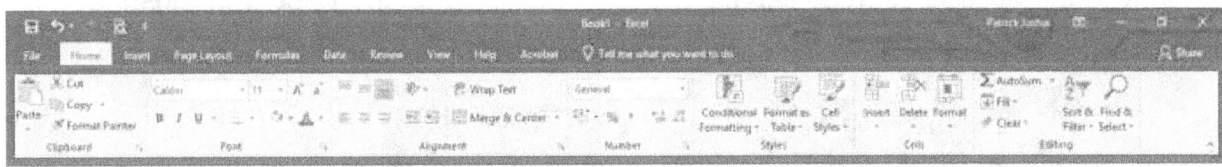 for frequently used features like Save, Undo, or Print Preview can be customised.

Home Menu - are employed to carry out a number of tasks, like changing fonts, aligning text, inserting rows, etc.

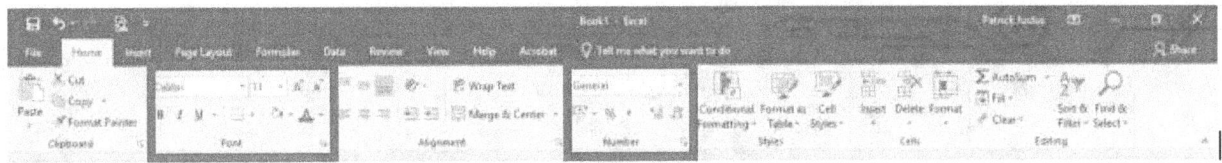

Ribbons - are arranged into **Data Groups** of related tasks, such as the Font or Alignment group.

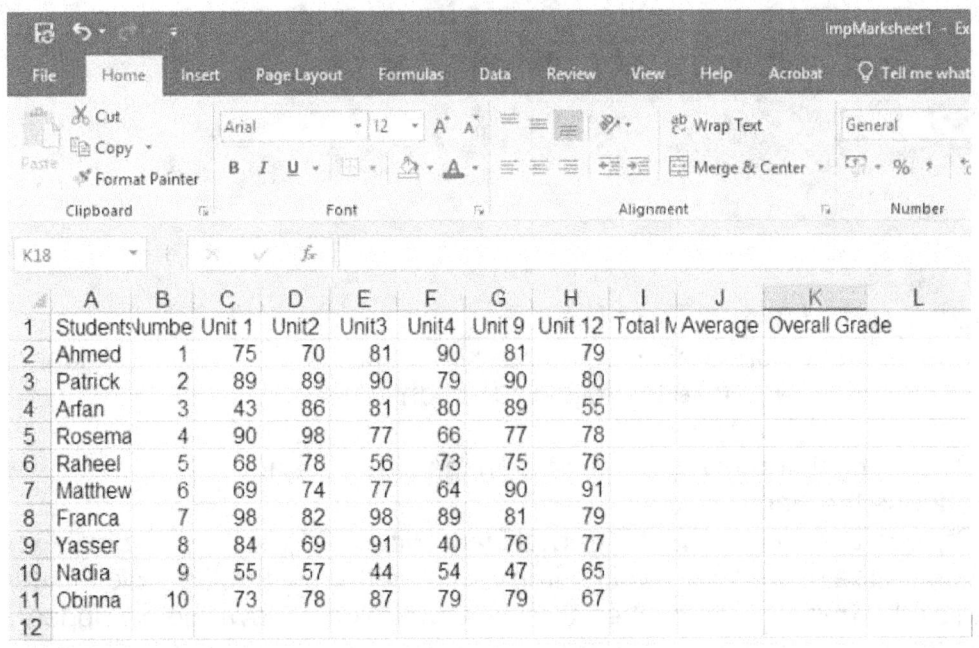

Step 2: Creating the Mark Sheet Spreadsheet

Carefully type in the information in the spreadsheet below, making sure to enter the data 'as is' in the appropriate cells as indicated below.

Alternately, if a source is provided and the spreadsheet file (ImpMarksheet1.xlsx) is accessible, you may download, import, or copy the contents to your computer before opening the data in your spreadsheet workbook:

	A	B	C	D	E	F	G	H	I	J	K	L
1	Students	Numbe	Unit 1	Unit2	Unit3	Unit4	Unit 9	Unit 12	Total M	Average	Overall Grade	
2	Ahmed	1	75	70	81	90	81	79				
3	Patrick	2	89	89	90	79	90	80				
4	Arfan	3	43	86	81	80	89	55				
5	Rosema	4	90	98	77	66	77	78				
6	Raheel	5	68	78	56	73	75	76				
7	Matthew	6	69	74	77	64	90	91				
8	Franca	7	98	82	98	89	81	79				
9	Yasser	8	84	69	91	40	76	77				
10	Nadia	9	55	57	44	54	47	65				
11	Obinna	10	73	78	87	79	79	67				
12												

*Fig.3: Unformatted Excel Spreadsheet – **ImpMarksheet1.xlsx***

Import Data into Spreadsheet

There are numerous data imports available for Excel spreadsheets. You can import data from a variety of sources, including Microsoft Access, the web, text/CSV files, and other sources listed below, including SQL Server, Analysis Services, OData Data Feeds, XML Data Import, Data Connection Wizard, and Microsoft Query.

To Import Data:
Any of the desired sources can be chosen by clicking on the Excel Spreadsheet Data menu:

To import data from a Text file

If available; find the stored text file (impMarksheet.txt) in the specified folder, for instance, DataFiles, and take the following actions:

   i. Open a fresh, empty spreadsheet (in the usual way)
   ii. Choose the Home cell, A1
   iii. Choose Data menu | Get External Data Ribbon (if visible), | From Text
   iv. Locate the necessary text file (impMarksheet.txt) in the DataFiles folder and click the **Import** button when the dialogue box as shown below appears:

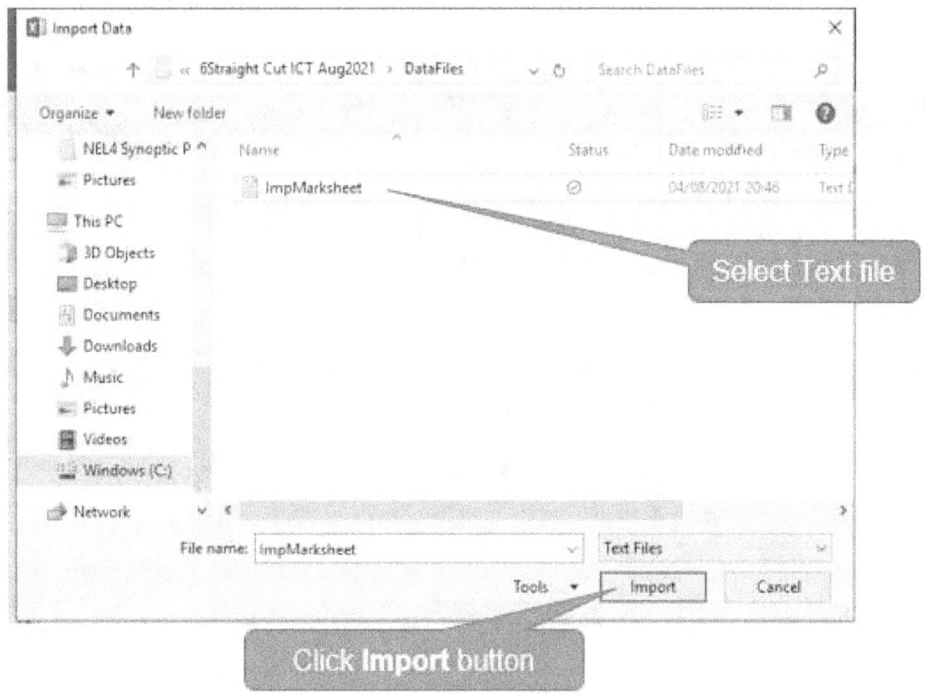

v.   A new dialogue box—the "Text Import Wizard"—that can recognise the different sorts of data in the spreadsheet that is being used and displayed, will emerge as shown. The default selection will be Comma Delimiter since it is the standard for data separation. If the delimiter in your data differs from the one in the example, choose it from the picklist under Delimiter:

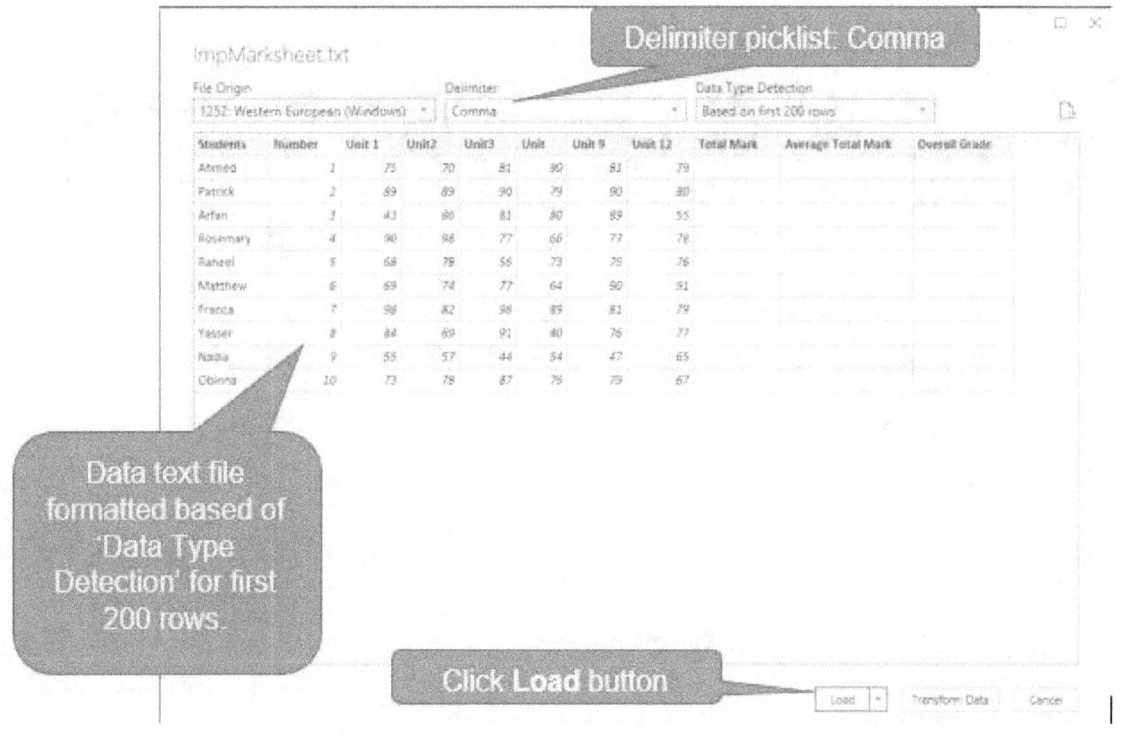

vi. After you click the Load button in the dialogue box labelled "Data Import Preview Data" above, the new spreadsheet data will be imported and shown as indicated in the Design menu window of the spreadsheet (in a new sheet tab):

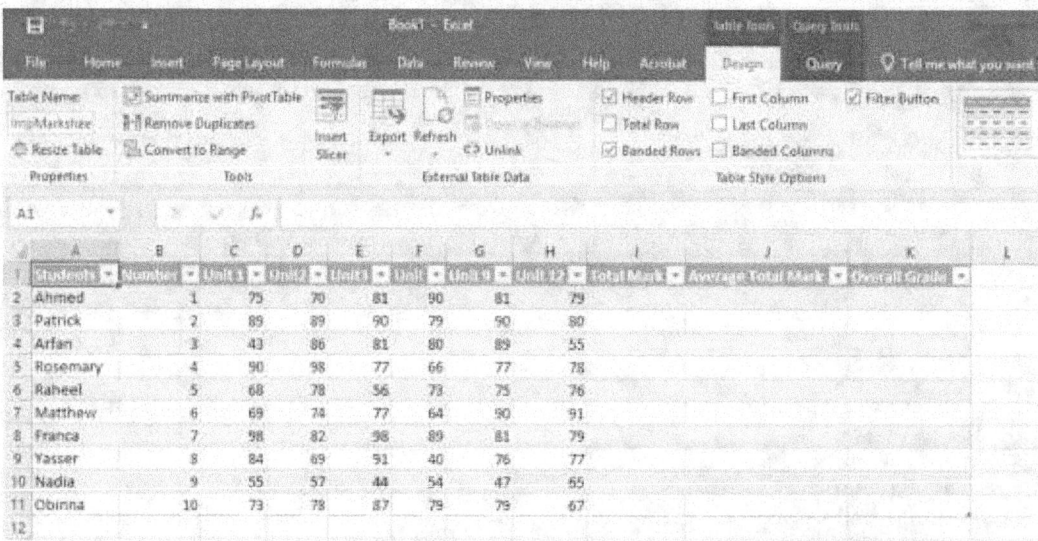

vii. vii. The spreadsheet should now have the imported data in a new sheet tab.

viii. The imported spreadsheet has undergone some suggestive and automated formatting, as seen in item vii. We must style the spreadsheet appropriately if we want to change or customise the data in any way. A particular amount of actions must be taken in order to format the spreadsheet; for instructions on formatting the spreadsheet, see step 3 below.

ix. If the data has been properly imported, formatted, (copied, downloaded, or written in), you should have a spreadsheet that resembles the illustration in Fig. 3 below:

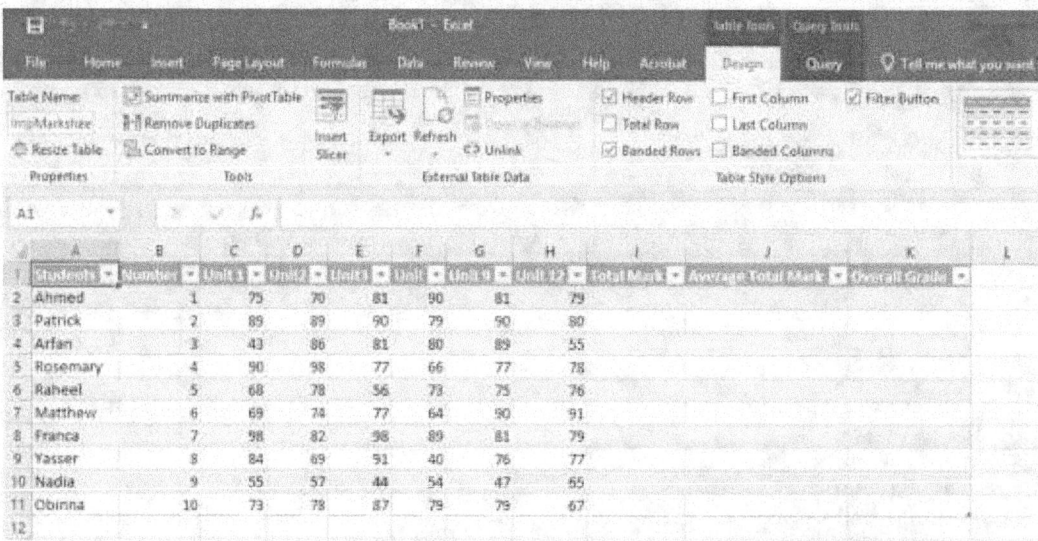

Fig.3: Part Formatted Excel Spreadsheet

x. Give the spreadsheet a suitable filename, such as ImpMarksheet2.xlsx, and then click the save icon to save the file to your desired location.

Step 3: Formatting the Spreadsheet

When formatting a spreadsheet, a variety of actions must be taken on the spreadsheet, including:

1. Make sure the spreadsheet prints on one page and that the page layout is landscape.
2. Bold all of the headings.
3. Ensure that all column headings are clear and readable.
4. Highlight the headers.
5. Make all of the spreadsheet's borders visible.
6. Check your spelling, text formatting, and font size.
7. Correctly format all data kinds (number, currency, date, percentage), and centre all data.
8. Adjust decimal values for all number, currency, and percentage data types as necessary.

Formatting Processes

Apply the formatting described above while paying close attention to the infographics below:

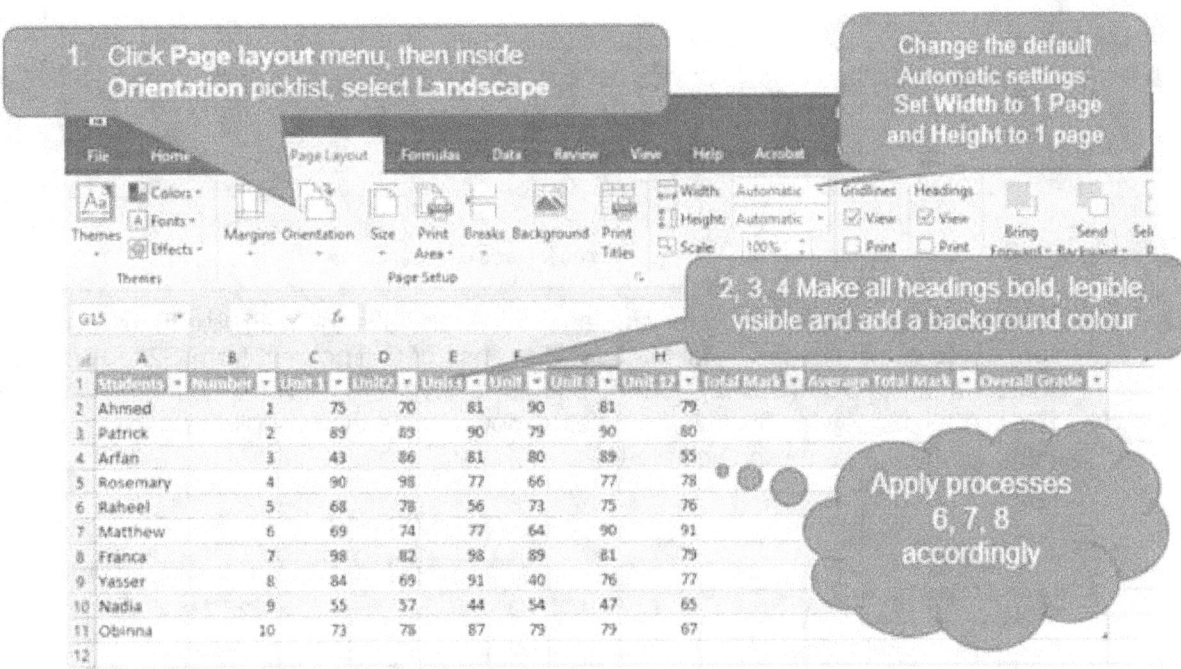

Fig. 4: Spreadsheet - Formatting processes from Step 3 above

Formatted Spreadsheet

The diagram below represents how a properly formatted spreadsheet should appear. To prevent unintentional data loss, always save your spreadsheet at regular intervals.

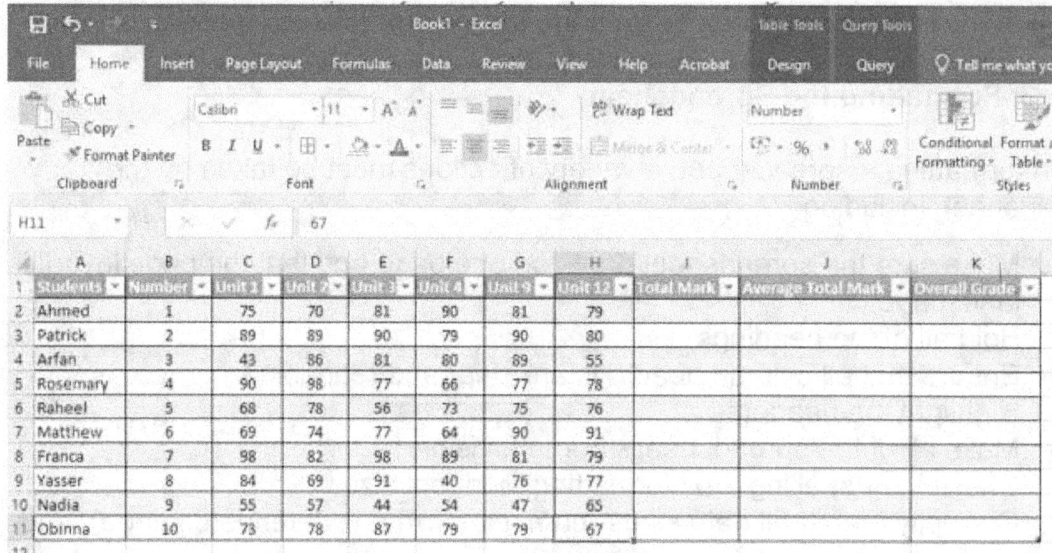

Fig.5: Formatted Excel Spreadsheet – saved as, **ImpMarksheet3.xlsx**

Step 4: Calculating the Total Mark

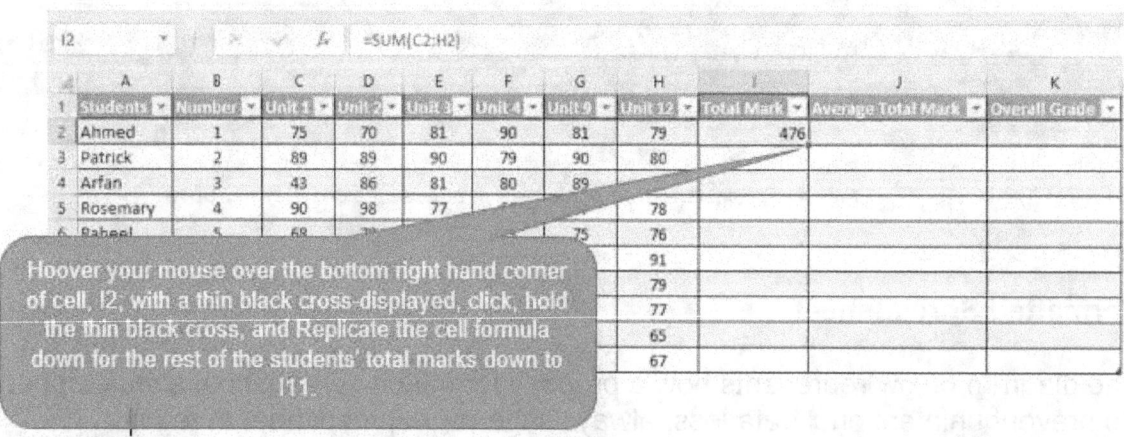

Fig. 6: The above diagram illustrates/identifies formatted parts of Excel Spreadsheet.

- Find cell I2 (column I, row 2) for student Ahmed and use the following function or formula to determine the Total Mark for his range of unit scores, from C2 to H2: Enter the command =SUM(C2:H2). Ahmed should receive a 476-overall score.
- Replicate i.e. copy the formula from cell I2 down to the other pupils as necessary, centring the data – as shown below:.

| | fₓ | =SUM(C2:H2) | | | | | | | | |

A	B	C	D	E	F	G	H	I	J	K
Students	Number	Unit 1	Unit 2	Unit 3	Unit 4	Unit 9	Unit 12	Total Mark	Average Total Mark	Overall Grade
Ahmed	1	75	70	81	90	81	79	476		
Patrick	2	89	89	90	79	90	80	517		
Arfan	3	43	86	81	80	89	55	434		
Rosemary	4	90	98	77	66	77	78	486		
Raheel	5	68	78	56	73	75	76	426		
Matthew	6	69	74	77	64	90	91	465		
Franca	7	98	82	98	89	81	79	527		
Yasser	8	84	69	91	40	76	77	437		
Nadia	9	55	57	44	54	47	65	322		
Obinna	10	73	78	87	79	79	67	463		

- Click the save icon to save/update the file.

Alternatively,

- The AutoSum icon contains shortcuts for the following functions: Total, Average, Count Numbers, Maximum, Minimum, and others:

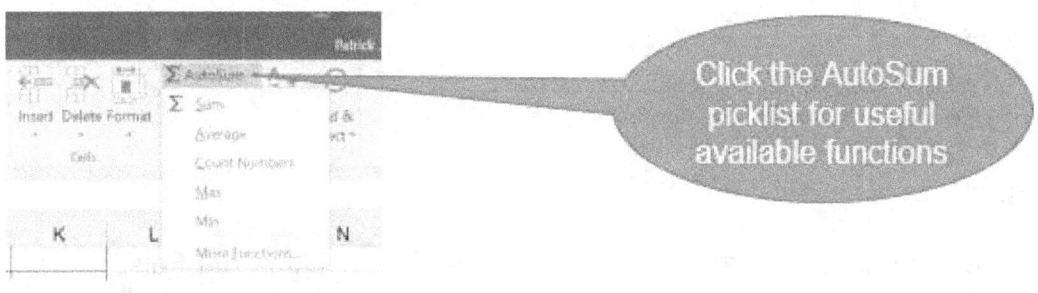

Click the AutoSum picklist for useful available functions

Step 5: Calculating the Average Total Mark

| SUM | × ✓ fₓ | =AVERAGE(C2:H2) | | | | | | | | |

A	B	C	D	E	F	G	H	I	J	K
Students	Number	Unit 1	Unit 2	Unit 3	Unit 4	Unit 9	Unit 12	Total Mark	Average Total Mark	Overall Grade
Ahmed	1	75	70	81	90	81	79	476	=AVERAGE(C2:H2)	
Patrick	2	89	89	90	79	90	80	517		
Arfan	3	43	86	81	80	89	55	434		
Rosemary	4	90	98	77	66	77	78	486		
Raheel	5	68	78	56	73	75	76	426		
Matthew	6	69	74	77	64	90	91	465		=Average(RangeOfCells)
Franca	7	98	82	98	89	81	79	527		
Yasser	8	84	69	91	40	76	77	437		
Nadia	9	55	57	44	54	47	65	322		
Obinna	10	73	78	87	79	79	67	463		

Fig. 7: The above diagram illustrates/identifies the Column J for the Average Total Mark.

- Locate cell J2 for student Ahmed and use the following function or formula to determine the Average Total Mark for his Unit Scores (C2 to H2):
  =AVERAGE(C2:H2)
- Centre the data and replicate the formula down to the other students as necessary.
- If not already indicated or modelled, format the Average Total Mark column to a whole number or as necessary.
- To save/update the file, click the save icon.

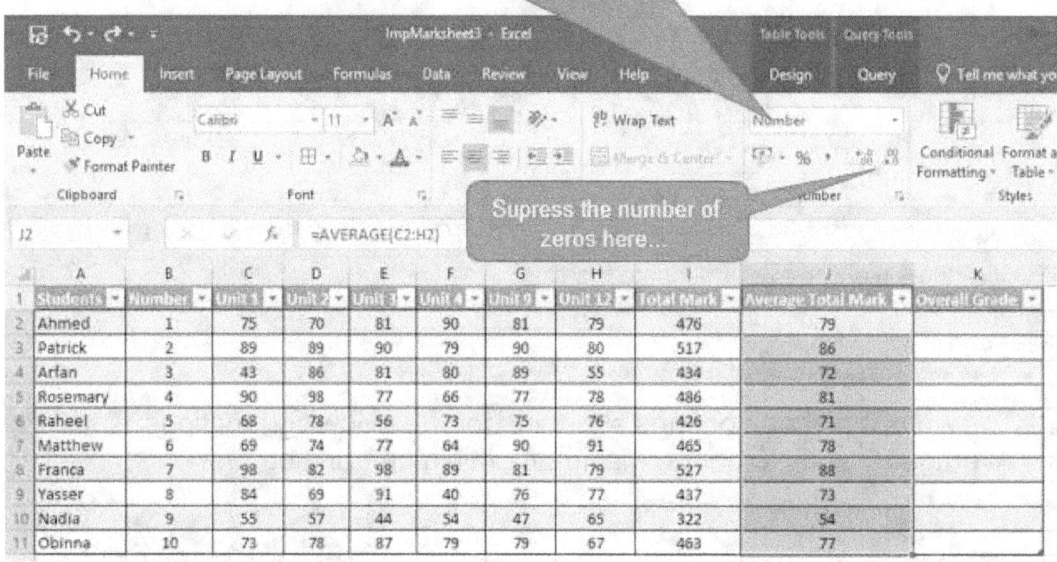

Fig. 8: The above diagram illustrates/identifies the Average Total Mark Column J; Select cells J2:J11, centre the data and format to whole number.

THE IF FUNCTION

(i)   The IF Function is expressed as follows: =IF(Condition,True,False)
      Recall that a condition is an argument or query that will be tested; if the test's outcome is true, True will be applied; otherwise, False will be applied. Important: Double quotes are placed above characters returned by IF functions, such as "Include." Unquoted numbers are returned in their unaltered state.

THE IF AND FUNCTION (IF OR FUNCTION)

Note: The **IF AND** function includes two conditions, Conditions 1 and 2, therefore treat them independently. Then, bracket the two conditions and separate them with a comma. Put an AND in front of the brackets as follows:

AND(Condition1, Condition2)

Similarly, the OR condition functions is like the AND condition by replacing the AND with an OR in the formula:

OR(Condition1, Condition2)

(ii) Next, replace **Condition** in (i) above with **AND(Condition1, Condition2)** and you will have:

=IF(AND(Condition1, Condition2), True, False); treat this function as normal.

(iii) For the **OR(Condition1, Condition2);**
replace **Condition** in (i) above with **OR(Condition1, Condition2)** and you will have:

=IF(OR(Condition1, Condition2), True, False); again, treat the function as normal.

Practice Activity

Use cases and applications for "IF Function", "Nested IF", "IF AND" and "IF OR"

- Generate the spreadsheet below using the identical cell coordinates:

Students	Number	Gender	Age	19 or less	25 or less	25 to 40	40 or more	over 35 and male	over 30 or female	over 30 and female
Ahmed	1	M	25							
Patrick	2	M	33							
Arfan	3	M	22							
Rosemary	4	F	40							
Raheel	5	M	32							
Matthew	6	M	18							
Franca	7	F	35							
Yasser	8	M	43							
Nadia	9	F	28							
Obinna	10	M	45							

Fig. 9: Using selection in Spreadsheet – IF Functions

- To begin with, you need a formula in E5 that will use D5 to perform a logical test to determine whether the students are 19 years old or younger (i.e., whether D5<=19).
- Enter the following formula in cell E5: =IF(D5<=19,D5,"")
- If D5's age is 19 or less and the test is valid, D5's age will be transferred into E5. A blank (" ") is shown in E5 if the age is more than 19, which renders the test invalid.
- The F5 requires a method similar to IF().
- The H5 requires a function similar to IF().

However;

- G5 will need a more complex formula since you want an outcome that is either true or false transferred into G5 if D5>=25 and D5=40. In this case, the AND() function inside the IF() function is what you need.
- For cells I5, J5, and K5, a similar function to that in G5 will be necessary; however, a second set of data will come from the gender cell C5. As a result, I5 will look for data in cell D5 that is over 35 and male, J5 will look for data in cell D5 that is over 30 or female, and K5 will look for data that is over 30 and female, respectively.
- When the above has been correctly finished or carried out, your spreadsheet should appear as follows:

	A	B	C	D	E	F	G	H	I	J	K
1	Using Selection in Spreadsheet										
2	IF, IF AND, IF OR Functions										
3											
4	Students	Number	Gender	Age	19 or less	25 or less	25 to 40	40 or more	over 35 and male	over 30 or female	over 30 and female
5	Ahmed	1	M	25		25	25				
6	Patrick	2	M	33			33			33	
7	Arfan	3	M	22		22					
8	Rosemary	4	F	40			40	40		40	40
9	Raheel	5	M	32			32			32	
10	Matthew	6	M	18	18	18					
11	Franca	7	F	35			35			35	35
12	Yasser	8	M	43				43	43	43	
13	Nadia	9	F	28			28			28	
14	Obinna	10	M	45				45	45	45	

Fig. 10: Correctly completed Spreadsheet showcasing the IF, IF AND, IF OR Functions

Reminder:

- In order to pass the Level 2 Functional Skill ICT tests, you must use IF Statements in a spreadsheet.
- Pay close attention to its application and reasoning.
- Practice makes perfect.

Recall our earlier Marksheet Spreadsheet

Step 6: Calculating the Overall Grade

THE NESTED IF FUNCTION

The **nested IF** Function first looks for a true outcome from the specified sequence of results one after the other; if no true outcome is discovered, it produces a false result.

In this instance: The following comprises the overall grade criteria:

- Return "D" for Distinction if your score is 75 or higher
- Return "M" for Merit if your score is 60 or higher;
- Return "P" for Pass if your score is 40 or higher; and
- Return "F" for Fail if your score is lower.

This results in a nested IF scenario from which we will return the accurate grades.

*With the **Average Total Mark** in Cell J2:*

If the value in cell J2 is more than or equal to 75 (denoted by >= 75), we will return a "D" for Distinction and, if true, instead of returning True at this point, we will continue to test whether true on other average total marks for all grades D, M, and P. If the argument or query cannot produce a true result, it will instead return a False result, or a grade of "F".

The complete nested IF function is shown below:

=IF(J2>=75,"D",IF(J2>=60,"M",IF(J2>=40,"P","F")))

You'll see that we used closing brackets to close all of the opened brackets, so there are three open and three closed brackets. The equal symbol (=) indicates to the spreadsheet that a formula or function is being used.

- Choose student Ahmed's cell K2 and enter the following function to get Ahmed's overall grade based on his average total mark score. Don't rush this step and take your time to comprehend the function's reasoning.
  =IF(J2>=75,"D",IF(J2>=60,"M",IF(J2>=40,"P","F")))
- Centre the data and replicate the formula down to the other students as necessary.
- To save/update the file, click on the save icon.

=IF(J2>=75,"D",IF(J2>=60,"M",IF(J2>=40,"P","F")))

K2			fx	=IF(J2>=75,"D",IF(J2>=60,"M",IF(J2>=40,"P","F")))						
	A	B	C	D	E	F	G	H	I	J	K
1	Students	Number	Unit 1	Unit 2	Unit 3	Unit 4	Unit 9	Unit 12	Total Mark	Average Total Mark	Overall Grade
2	Ahmed	1	75	70	81	90	81	79	476	79	D
3	Patrick	2	89	89	90	79	90	80	517	86	
4	Arfan	3	43	86	81	80	89	55	434	72	
5	Rosemary	4	90	98	77	66	77	78	486	81	
6	Raheel	5	68	78	56	73	75	76	426	71	
7	Matthew	6	69	74	77	64	90	91	465	78	
8	Franca	7	98	82	98	89	81	79	527	88	
9	Yasser	8	84	69	91	40	76	77	437	73	
10	Nadia	9	55	57	44	54	47	65	322	54	
11	Obinna	10	73	78	87	79	79	67	463	77	

Fig. 11: Calculating the Overall Grade – using a Nested IF Function

Step 7: Finished Spreadsheet

- After correctly completing steps 3, 4, and 5, you should have the spreadsheet displayed in the infographics below:

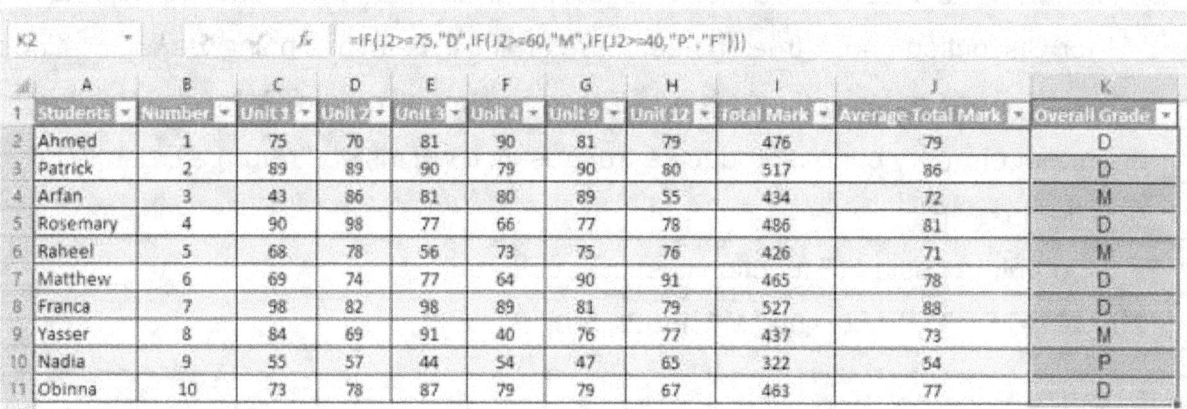

K2			fx	=IF(J2>=75,"D",IF(J2>=60,"M",IF(J2>=40,"P","F")))						
	A	B	C	D	E	F	G	H	I	J	K
1	Students	Number	Unit 1	Unit 2	Unit 3	Unit 4	Unit 9	Unit 12	Total Mark	Average Total Mark	Overall Grade
2	Ahmed	1	75	70	81	90	81	79	476	79	D
3	Patrick	2	89	89	90	79	90	80	517	86	D
4	Arfan	3	43	86	81	80	89	55	434	72	M
5	Rosemary	4	90	98	77	66	77	78	486	81	D
6	Raheel	5	68	78	56	73	75	76	426	71	M
7	Matthew	6	69	74	77	64	90	91	465	78	D
8	Franca	7	98	82	98	89	81	79	527	88	D
9	Yasser	8	84	69	91	40	76	77	437	73	M
10	Nadia	9	55	57	44	54	47	65	322	54	P
11	Obinna	10	73	78	87	79	79	67	463	77	D

Fig. 12: Finished Spreadsheet - where steps 3, 4, 5 and 6 are correctly completed.

SORTING THE SPREADSHEET

Step 8: Sorting the Spreadsheet

Do the following to order the spreadsheet from largest to smallest (descending order) and sort by the average total mark:

• Choose the spreadsheet with headings (i.e., range A1:K11) - see infographics below:

A1				f_x	Students						
	A	B	C	D	E	F	G	H	I	J	K
1	Students	Number	Unit 1	Unit 2	Unit 3	Unit 4	Unit 9	Unit 12	Total Mark	Average Total Mark	Overall Grade
2	Ahmed	1	75	70	81	90	81	79	476	79	D
3	Patrick	2	89	89	90	79	90	80	517	86	D
4	Arfan	3	43	86	81	80	89	55	434	72	M
5	Rosemary	4	90	98	77	66	77	78	486	81	D
6	Raheel	5	68	78	56	73	75	76	426	71	M
7	Matthew	6	69	74	77	64	90	91	465	78	D
8	Franca	7	98	82	98	89	81	79	527	88	D
9	Yasser	8	84	69	91	40	76	77	437	73	M
10	Nadia	9	55	57	44	54	47	65	322	54	P
11	Obinna	10	73	78	87	79	79	67	463	77	D

- Click the **Data** menu bar and choose **Sort** from the **Sort & Filter** ribbon.:

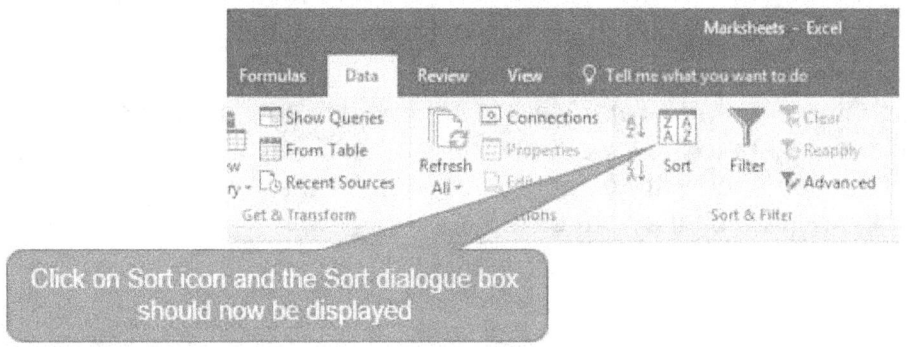

- The Sort dialogue box should now be displayed:

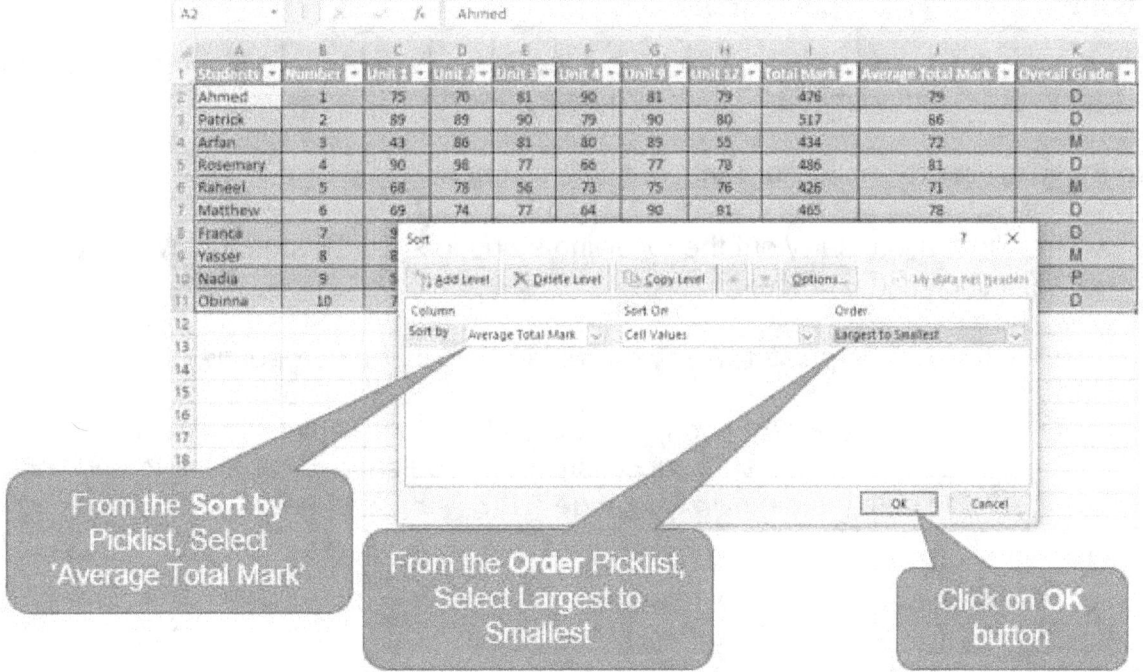

- The **Sorted** spreadsheet result is as shown below:

	A	B	C	D	E	F	G	H	I	J	K
1	Students	Number	Unit 1	Unit 2	Unit 3	Unit 4	Unit 9	Unit 12	Total Mark	Average Total Mark	Overall Grade
2	Franca	7	98	82	98	89	81	79	527	88	D
3	Patrick	2	89	89	90	79	90	80	517	86	D
4	Rosemary	4	90	98	77	66	77	78	486	81	D
5	Ahmed	1	75	70	81	90	81	79	476	79	D
6	Matthew	6	69	74	77	64	90	91	465	78	D
7	Obinna	10	73	78	87	79	79	67	463	77	D
8	Yasser	8	84	69	91	40	76	77	437	73	M
9	Arfan	3	43	86	81	80	89	55	434	72	M
10	Raheel	5	68	78	56	73	75	76	426	71	M
11	Nadia	9	55	57	44	54	47	65	322	54	P

Fig. 13: Sorted Spreadsheet – sorted by column J, Average Total Mark

You'll see that the Average Total Mark in column J is now presented top down, going from the highest mark to the lowest mark. All other data in the spreadsheet are displayed in accordance with the criteria defined for the Average Total Mark, which is the only column in which they are displayed.

FILTERING THE SPREADSHEET

Step 9: Filtering the Spreadsheet

Filters are used to get specific data (or a specific set of data) from a spreadsheet that satisfy specific requirements. Filters can be applied to one or more criteria.

Do the following to apply filters with a single criterion:

- For illustration, carry out the following steps to show all students who received a Distinction (D) grade:

  o Move the pointer to any cell or heading in the spreadsheet.

  o Select the Filter option from the Data menu (depicted by a funnel). Performing this step successfully will add choose list icons to each of the data headings in the range A1: K1, as seen below:

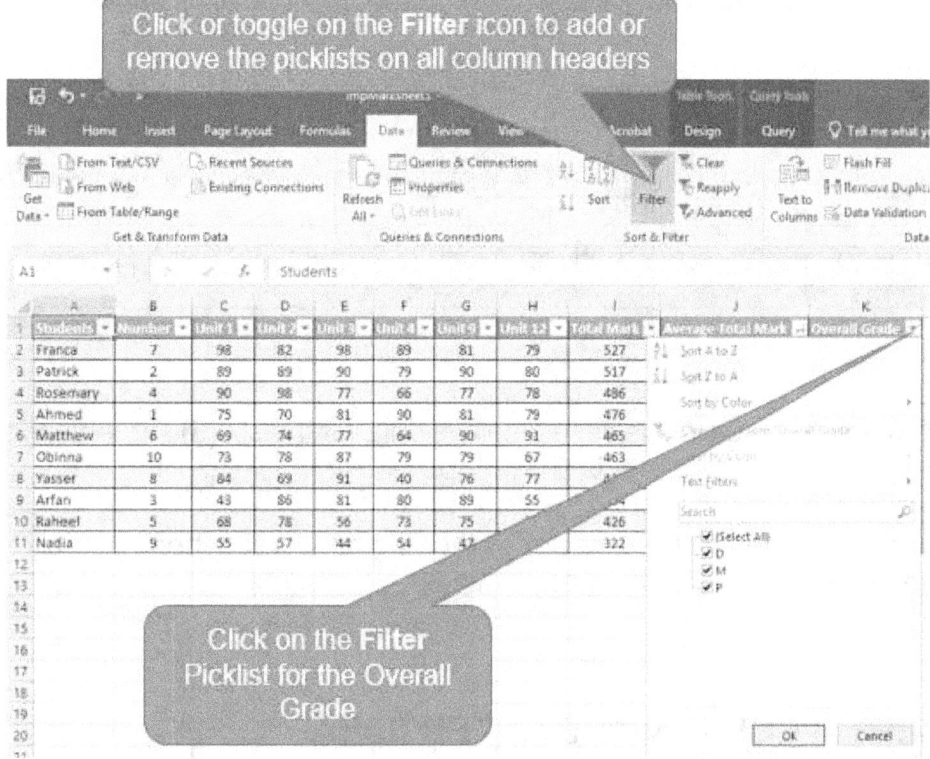

- After selecting the filter check box in cell K1 (Overall Grade), a drop-down list will appear with all available and checked grades as indicated in the above image.

- Check only the Distinction (D) grade and leave the remaining checkboxes and Select All unchecked (see infographics below):

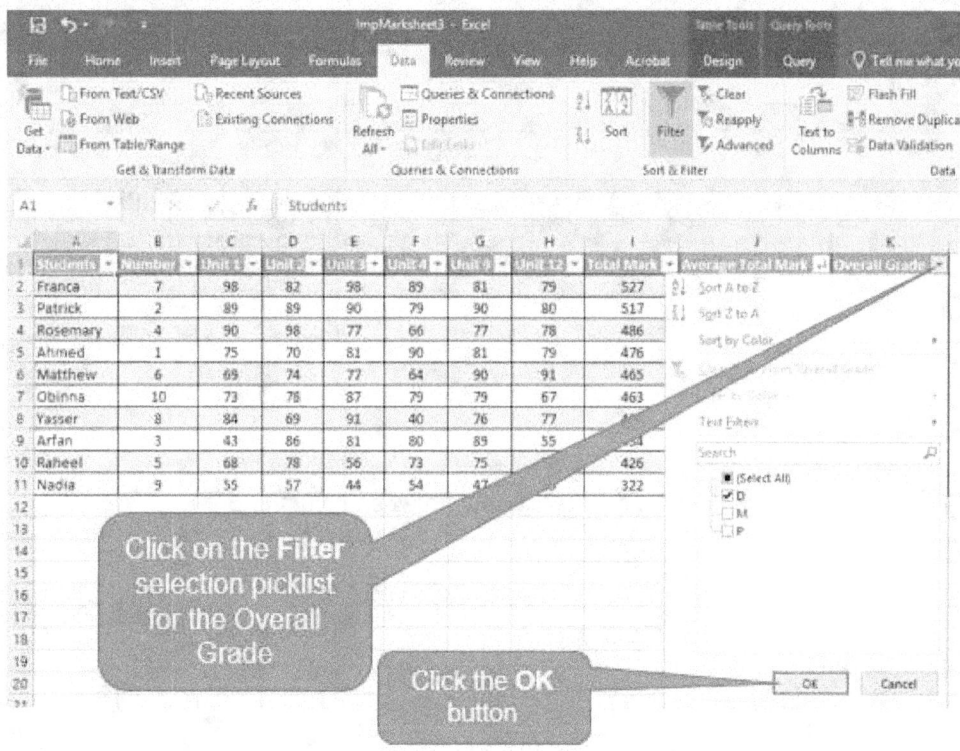

- Next, press **OK**. The filtered results should now only show information for students who received an overall Distinction (D) grade, as shown below:

	A	B	C	D	E	F	G	H	I	J	K
	Students	Number	Unit 1	Unit 2	Unit 3	Unit 4	Unit 9	Unit 12	Total Mark	Average Total Mark	Overall Grade
2	Franca	7	98	82	98	89	81	79	527	88	D
3	Patrick	2	89	89	90	79	90	80	517	86	D
4	Rosemary	4	90	98	77	66	77	78	486	81	D
5	Ahmed	1	75	70	81	90	81	79	476	79	D
6	Matthew	6	69	74	77	64	90	91	465	78	D
7	Obinna	10	73	78	87	79	79	67	463	77	D

Cell reference: A1 — Students

The filtered result, which in this case displays data for the six (6) students that received an overall distinction (D) grade, is shown above.

- To remove the filter and return to the original spreadsheet, just click the **Data** menu | **Filter** icon once more.

TO INSERT A COLUMN AND ENTER DATA

Step 10: Inserting a Column and Entering data into the Spreadsheet

Column C can be highlighted or selected, and then by performing a right-click, a shortcut menu list is displayed; The contents of column C will be moved to column D when you choose insert, leaving column C empty as illustrated in fig. 14:

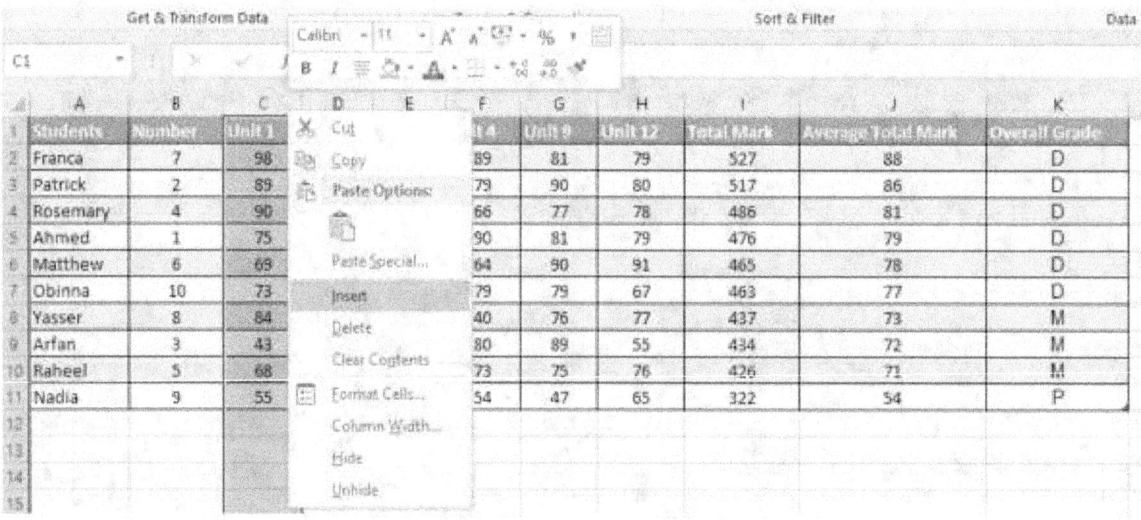

Fig. 14: Inserting a new column in a Spreadsheet between columns B and C.

Relative Cell Referencing

Formula in columns I, J, K changes **relatively** to columns J, K, L, their results remain the same.

	A	B	C	D	E	F	G	H	I	J	K	L
1	Students	Number	Column1	Unit 1	Unit 2	Unit 3	Unit 4	Unit 9	Unit 12	Total Mark	Average Total Mark	Overall Grade
2	Franca	7		98	82	98	89	81	79	527	88	D
3	Patrick	2		89	89	90	79	90	80	517	86	D
4	Rosemary	4		90	98	77	66	77	78	486	81	D
5	Ahmed	1		75	70	81	90	81	79	476	79	D
6	Matthew	6		69	74	77	64	90	91	465	78	D
7	Obinna	10		73	78	87	79	79	67	463	77	D
8	Yasser	8		84	69	91	40	76	77	437	73	M
9	Arfan	3		43	86	81	80	89	55	434	72	M
10	Raheel	5		68	78	56	73	75	76	426	71	M
11	Nadia	9			57	44	54	47	65	322	54	P

Fig. 15: Inserted new column C in a Spreadsheet.

New column C (Column1) added between columns B and D

- Now, fill in the data in the newly created, empty column C.
- Change Column 1's placeholder name to Gender so that it serves as the column C's heading.
- Randomly assign a gender to each student, using the letters "M" for men and "F" for women.

	A	B	C	D	E	F	G	H	I	J	K	L
1	Students	Number	Gender	Unit 1	Unit 2	Unit 3	Unit 4	Unit 9	Unit 12	Total Mark	Average Total Mark	Overall Grade
2	Franca	7	F	98	82	98	89	81	79	527	88	D
3	Patrick	2	M	89	89	90	79	90	80	517	86	D
4	Rosemary	4	F	90	98	77	66	77	78	486	81	D
5	Ahmed	1	M	75	70	81	90	81	79	476	79	D
6	Matthew	6	M	69	74	77	64	90	91	465	78	D
7	Obinna	10	M	73	78	87	79	79	67	463	77	D
8	Yasser	8	M	84	69	91	40	76	77	437	73	M
9	Arfan	3	M	43	86	81	80	89	55	434	72	M
10	Raheel	5	M	68	78	56	73	75	76	426	71	M
11	Nadia	9	F	55	57	44	54	47	65	322	54	P

Fig. 16: Gender data added to Column C in the Spreadsheet.

Data Validation
Step 11: Validating Data

To limit the kind of data or values that users can enter into an Excel spreadsheet, utilise data validation rules. One of the most popular data validation methods is to establish a drop-down list with a small number of data options.

With Excel spreadsheets, the following data validation types are possible:

Data Validation Types	Descriptions
Whole number	Entries must only be whole numbers.
Decimal	Limit entries to decimal (%) values.
Departments	Limit choices to a list of options
Cost centres table	Table for Cost Centre List Source
Cost centre budget	Only allow choices from the Cost Centre list
Date	Limit entries to dates within a range
Time	Limit entries between a time frame
Text length	Limit entries to a certain number of characters
HR Budget	Limit entries to a certain maximum amount
Products	Require entries to meet certain text guidelines
Age verification	Limit entries below a certain age
Custom values	Limit entries to unique values only (no repeated entries)
E-Mail	Require entries to contain the @ symbol

Do the following to practise data validation using, for instance, whole numbers to limit entries into the mark sheet:

With the Mark Sheet spreadsheet open, verify that all value entries in Columns D to I have a minimum mark of 0 and a maximum mark of 100. – do the following:

- Choose the range of cells; D2:I14

- From the Data menu ribbon, choose the Data menu option, and then choose Data Validation from the picklist.

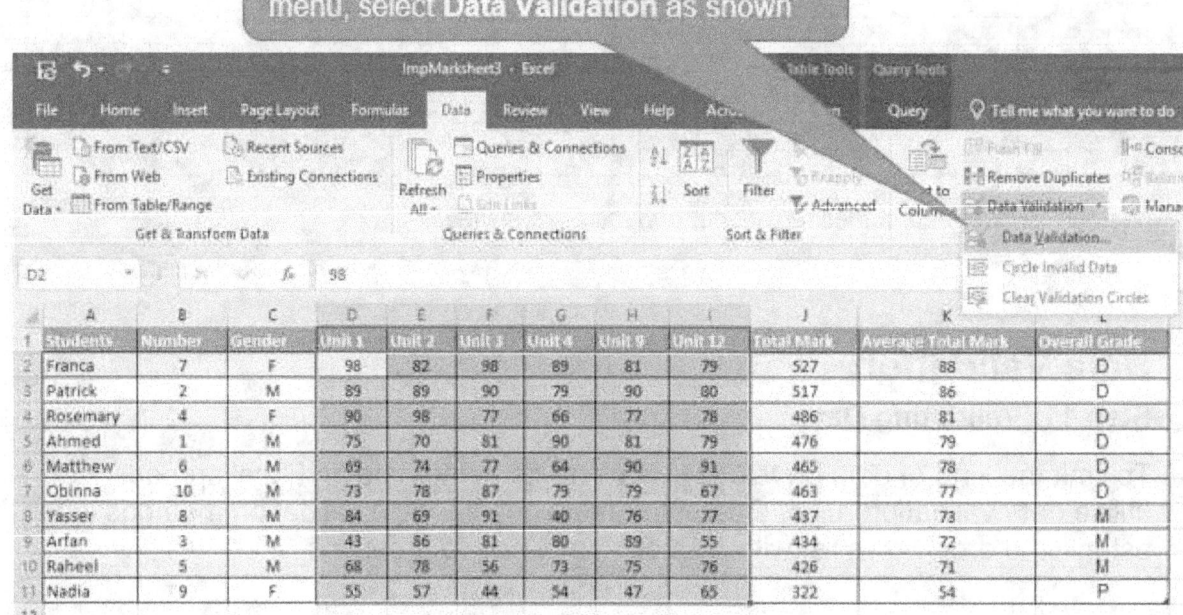

- If the instructions are correctly followed, the following data validation dialogue box will appear:

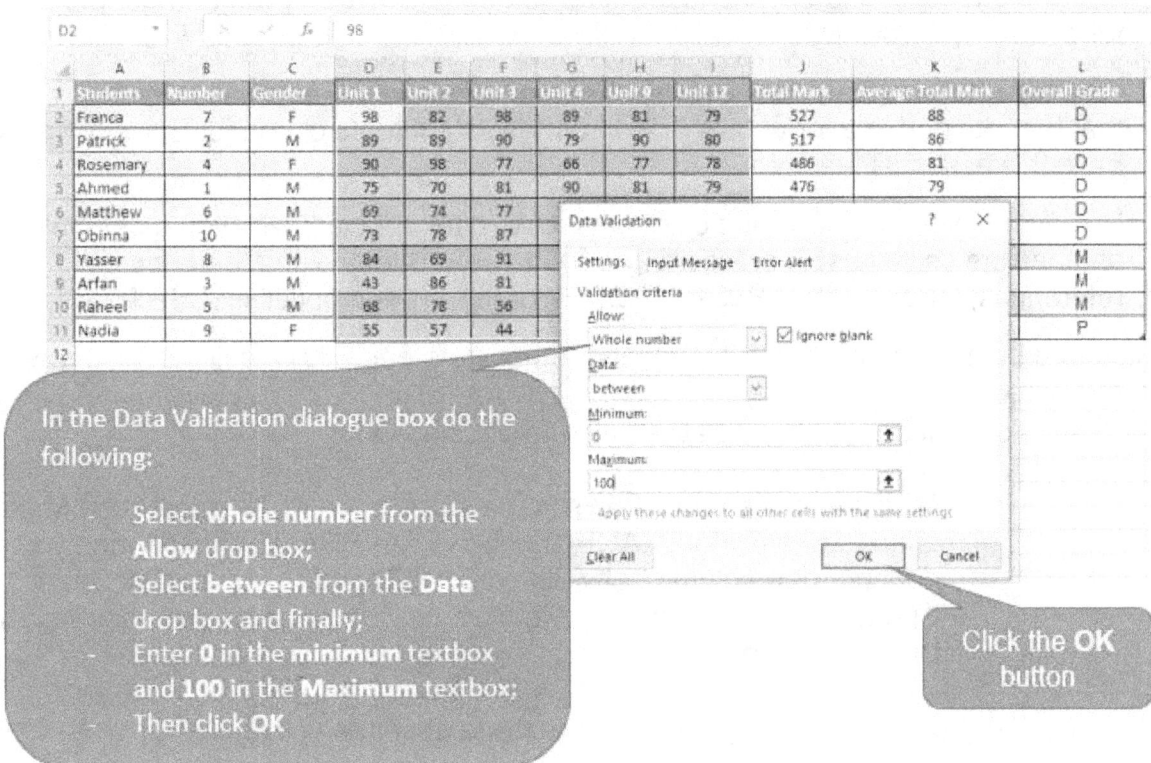

In the Data Validation dialogue box do the following:

- Select **whole number** from the **Allow** drop box;
- Select **between** from the **Data** drop box and finally;
- Enter **0** in the **minimum** textbox and **100** in the **Maximum** textbox;
- Then click **OK**

Click the **OK** button

Any number (such as 900) outside the range of 0 and 100 inclusive, or any other text or characters, will result in the display of an error message warning that "The value entered does not match the data validation defined for the cell" and requiring correction, retrying, or cancelling. An example of such a message is shown in the example error message below:

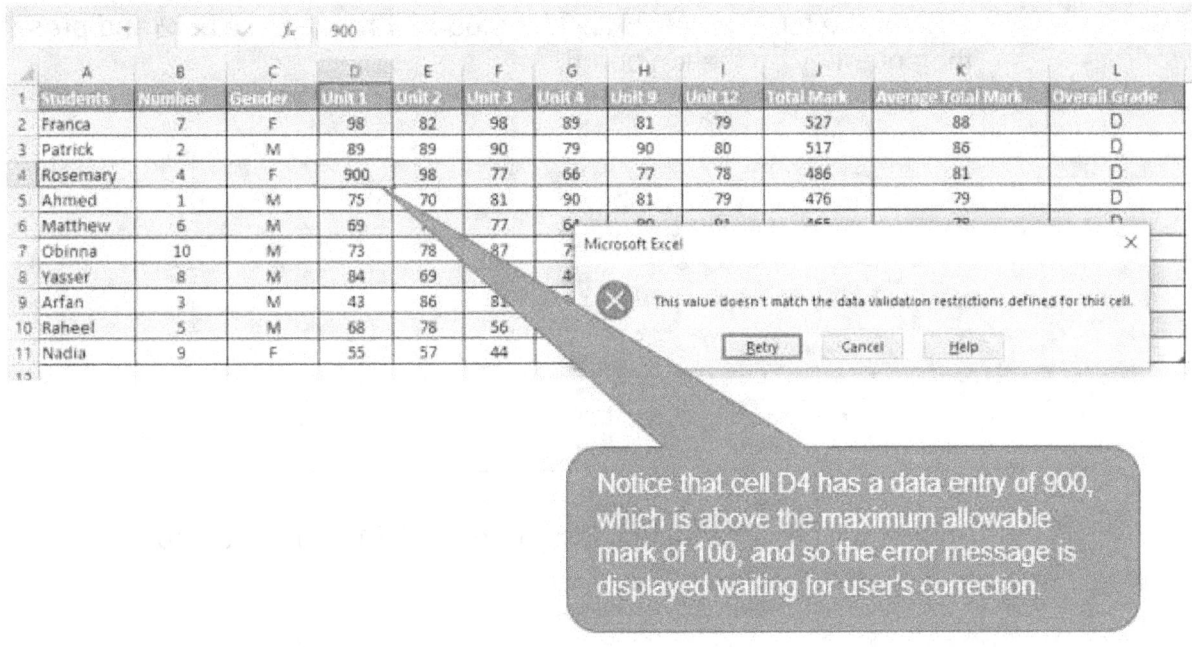

Notice that cell D4 has a data entry of 900, which is above the maximum allowable mark of 100, and so the error message is displayed waiting for user's correction.

Relative vs Absolute Cell Referencing

Step 12: Understanding Relative and Absolute Cell Referencing

A cell is often identified by the letter of its column, followed by the number of its row, for example, B3 or AD25.

Relative referencing in the formula will adjust to reflect the new cell reference if a cell that is contained in a formula is moved or has its contents changed. Spreadsheets have this essential feature.

However, if you do not want a cell's content to alter substantially, you must make it an absolute cell by using or inserting a $ sign before the column and row cell references, for example, $B$3 or $AD$25, or for a range of cells, $D$2:$I$11.

Before being used in a formula, naming (or giving a name to) a cell can also make it absolute.

- To demonstrate how relative cell referencing works:

    o Notice how the range fields in the formula under Average Total Mark changed from =AVERAGE(C2:H2) to =AVERAGE(D2:I2) when you added a new column between columns B and C in the Mark Sheet Spreadsheet (from above). Relative cell reference is demonstrated by that procedure.

- Carry out the following actions to illustrate absolute cell referencing:

    o Add a new column, M, and give it the title "% Achievement." To calculate the percentage achievement for column M, you must first add up the students' average total marks. Enter the sum in cell K12.

    o You must divide each student's average overall mark by the total of all average overall marks determined in cell K12 in order to determine each student's percent achievement.

    o o Enter the formula "=K2/K12" for student Franca in cell M2 and press the enter key on the keyboard:

SUM			X	✓	fx	=K2/K12						
	A	B	C	D	E	F	G	H	I	J	K	L	M
1	Students	Number	Gender	Unit 1	Unit 2	Unit 3	Unit 4	Unit 6	Unit 12	Total Mark	Average Total Mark	Overall Grade	% Achievement
2	Franca	7	F	98	82	98	89	81	75	527	88	D	=K2/K12
3	Patrick	2	M	89	89	90	79	90	80	517	86	D	
4	Rosemary	4	F	90	98	77	66	77	78	486	81	D	
5	Ahmed	1	M	75	70	81	90	81	79	476	79	D	
6	Matthew	6	M	65	74	77	64	90	91	465	78	D	
7	Obinna	10	M	73	78	87	79	79	67	463	77	D	
8	Yasser	8	M	84	69	91	40	76	77	437	73	M	
9	Arfan	3	M	43	86	81	80	89	55	434	72	M	
10	Raheel	5	M	68	78	56	73	75	76	426	71	M	
11	Nadia	9	F	55	57	44	54	47	65	322	54	P	
12											759		

    o Franca will get a 12% success rate on Cell M2 (formatted to percentage whole number)

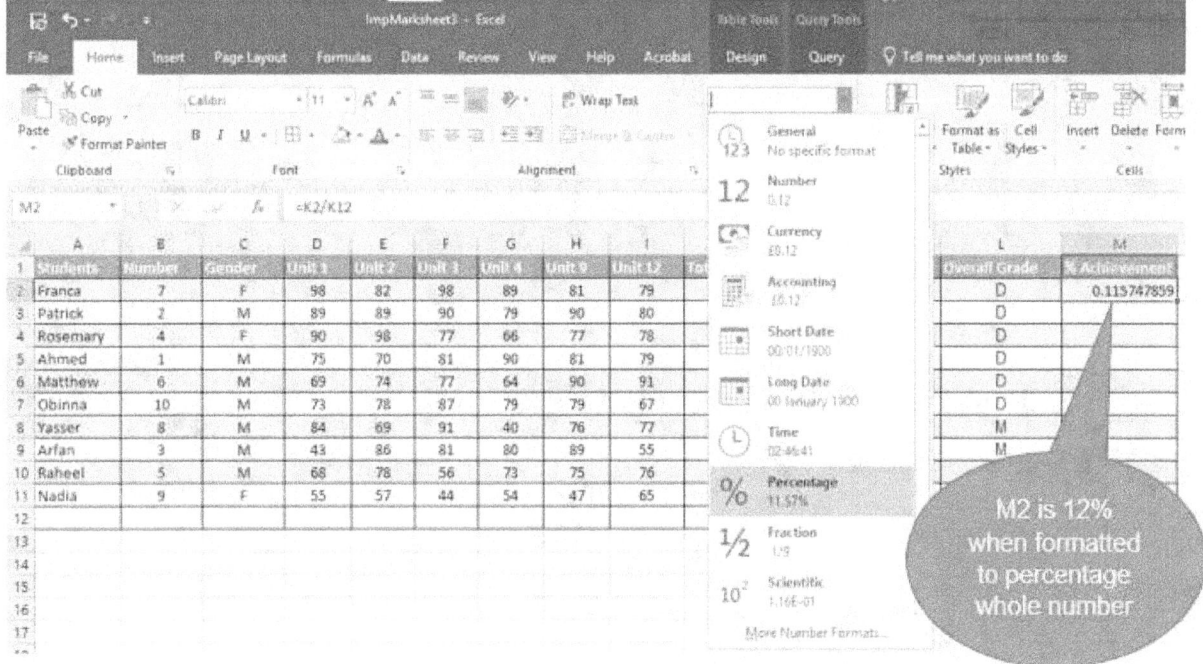

- You will receive the error "#DIV/0!" (division by zero) in the cells when you try to replicate the formula in cells M2 through M11; however, if you check or closely examine the cells, you will discover that the formula was actually dividing relatively by cells K13 through K21, which contained nothing (i.e. 0).

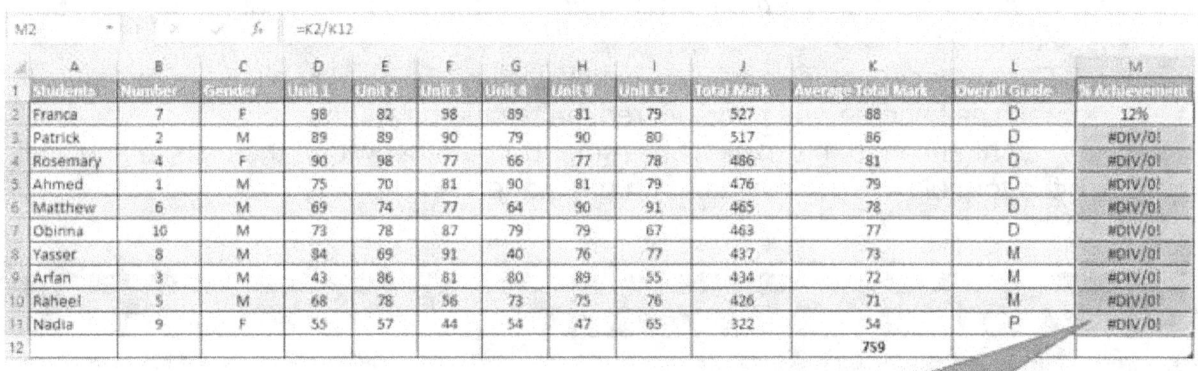

Rendering the **Absolute Cell Referencing** will fix the error, thus;

- Replace "=K2/K12" in cell M2 with "=K2/$K$12" by inserting the $ symbol in the divisor.

- Select M2 again and copy (or replicate) this new formula down into cell M11, and the right "% Achievements" will be realised.

- Save/update the spreadsheet.

- If everything went according to plan, you should have a spreadsheet like the one below.

Finished Spreadsheet View

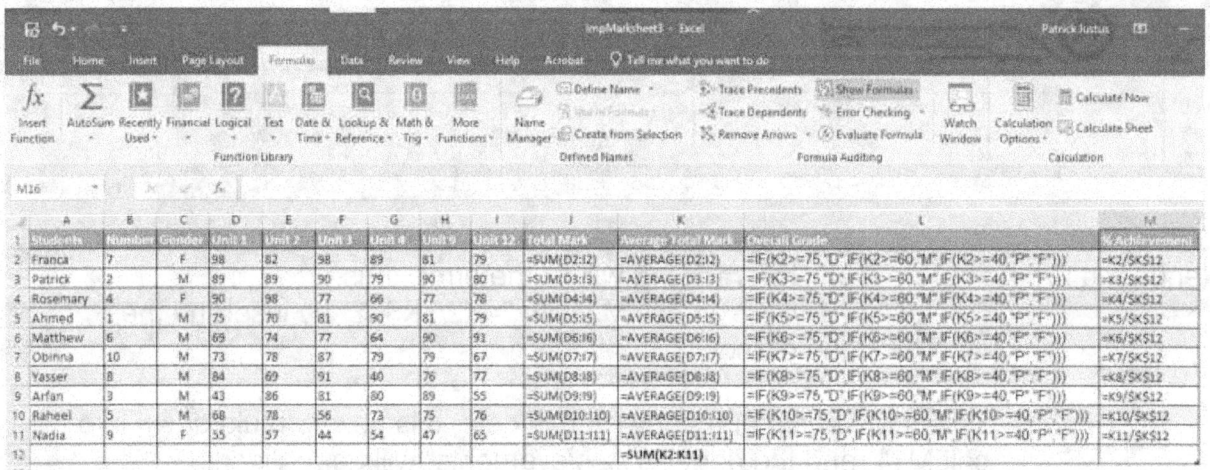

	A	B	C	D	E	F	G	H	I	J	K	L	M
1	Students	Number	Gender	Unit 1	Unit 2	Unit 3	Unit 4	Unit 9	Unit 12	Total Mark	Average Total Mark	Overall Grade	% Achievement
2	Franca	7	F	98	82	98	89	81	79	527	88	D	12%
3	Patrick	2	M	89	89	90	79	90	80	517	86	D	11%
4	Rosemary	4	F	90	98	77	66	77	78	486	81	D	11%
5	Ahmed	1	M	75	70	81	90	81	79	476	79	D	10%
6	Matthew	6	M	69	74	77	64	90	91	465	78	D	10%
7	Obinna	10	M	73	78	87	79	79	67	463	77	D	10%
8	Yasser	8	M	84	69	91	40	76	77	437	73	M	10%
9	Arfan	3	M	43	86	81	80	89	55	434	72	M	10%
10	Raheel	5	M	68	78	56	73	75	76	426	71	M	9%
11	Nadia	9	F	55	57	44	54	47	65	322	54	P	7%
12											759		

Fig. 17: Finished Spreadsheet View

> % Achievement now calculated using **Absolute** cell referencing

Formula View for the Finished Spreadsheet

Step 13: Viewing the Spreadsheet Formula

When the spreadsheet is complete, take the following actions to display the formula view:

- Click the Formula menu, then from the Formula Auditing ribbon, choose Show Formulas.
- The spreadsheet formula view is now visible. To display all of the formulas in each cell and on one page, increase the column widths.
- Pay attention to this exam requirement: You must widen the cells to show all the formula in each cell...and on one page.

	A	B	C	D	E	F	G	H	I	J	K	L	M
1	Students	Number	Gender	Unit 1	Unit 2	Unit 3	Unit 4	Unit 9	Unit 12	Total Mark	Average Total Mark	Overall Grade	% Achievement
2	Franca	7	F	98	82	98	89	81	79	=SUM(D2:I2)	=AVERAGE(D2:I2)	=IF(K2>=75,"D",IF(K2>=60,"M",IF(K2>=40,"P","F")))	=K2/$K$12
3	Patrick	2	M	89	89	90	79	90	80	=SUM(D3:I3)	=AVERAGE(D3:I3)	=IF(K3>=75,"D",IF(K3>=60,"M",IF(K3>=40,"P","F")))	=K3/$K$12
4	Rosemary	4	F	90	98	77	66	77	78	=SUM(D4:I4)	=AVERAGE(D4:I4)	=IF(K4>=75,"D",IF(K4>=60,"M",IF(K4>=40,"P","F")))	=K4/$K$12
5	Ahmed	1	M	75	70	81	90	81	79	=SUM(D5:I5)	=AVERAGE(D5:I5)	=IF(K5>=75,"D",IF(K5>=60,"M",IF(K5>=40,"P","F")))	=K5/$K$12
6	Matthew	6	M	69	74	77	64	90	91	=SUM(D6:I6)	=AVERAGE(D6:I6)	=IF(K6>=75,"D",IF(K6>=60,"M",IF(K6>=40,"P","F")))	=K6/$K$12
7	Obinna	10	M	73	78	87	79	79	67	=SUM(D7:I7)	=AVERAGE(D7:I7)	=IF(K7>=75,"D",IF(K7>=60,"M",IF(K7>=40,"P","F")))	=K7/$K$12
8	Yasser	8	M	84	69	91	40	76	77	=SUM(D8:I8)	=AVERAGE(D8:I8)	=IF(K8>=75,"D",IF(K8>=60,"M",IF(K8>=40,"P","F")))	=K8/$K$12
9	Arfan	3	M	43	86	81	80	89	55	=SUM(D9:I9)	=AVERAGE(D9:I9)	=IF(K9>=75,"D",IF(K9>=60,"M",IF(K9>=40,"P","F")))	=K9/$K$12
10	Raheel	5	M	68	78	56	73	75	76	=SUM(D10:I10)	=AVERAGE(D10:I10)	=IF(K10>=75,"D",IF(K10>=60,"M",IF(K10>=40,"P","F")))	=K10/$K$12
11	Nadia	9	F	55	57	44	54	47	65	=SUM(D11:I11)	=AVERAGE(D11:I11)	=IF(K11>=75,"D",IF(K11>=60,"M",IF(K11>=40,"P","F")))	=K11/$K$12
12											=SUM(K2:K11)		

Fig. 18: Finished Spreadsheet - Formula View

- To get back to the standard spreadsheet view, click on Show Formulas once more. Then, edit your spreadsheet columns once more to display all column headings and data properly.

Alternative method for showing formula view:

- On a **keyboard**, hold down the **Ctrl key** while pressing the key that is immediately to the left of the **1 key** to display the spreadsheet formula view.

- Press the same combination of keys to switch back to the standard spreadsheet view.

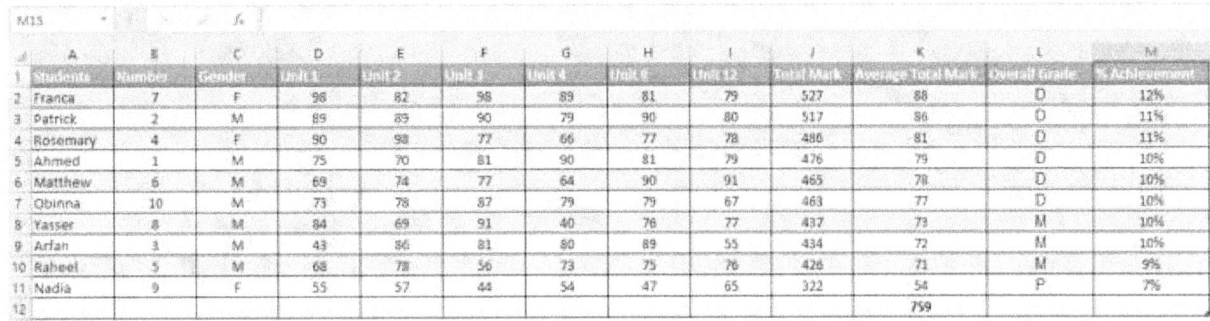

	A	B	C	D	E	F	G	H	I	J	K	L	M
1	Students	Number	Gender	Unit 1	Unit 2	Unit 3	Unit 4	Unit 6	Unit 12	Total Mark	Average Total Mark	Overall Grade	% Achievement
2	Franca	7	F	98	82	98	89	81	79	527	88	D	12%
3	Patrick	2	M	89	85	90	79	90	80	517	86	O	11%
4	Rosemary	4	F	90	98	77	66	77	78	486	81	D	11%
5	Ahmed	1	M	75	70	81	90	81	79	476	79	D	10%
6	Matthew	6	M	69	74	77	64	90	91	465	78	D	10%
7	Obinna	10	M	73	78	87	79	79	67	463	77	D	10%
8	Yasser	8	M	84	69	91	40	76	77	437	73	M	10%
9	Arfan	3	M	43	86	81	80	89	55	434	72	M	10%
10	Raheel	5	M	68	78	56	73	75	76	426	71	M	9%
11	Nadia	9	F	55	57	44	54	47	65	322	54	P	7%
12											759		

Fig. 19: Finished Spreadsheet - Normal View

GENERATING A CHART

Step 14: Generating a Spreadsheet Chart

To create a chart from the spreadsheet of each student's average total marks, present the chart alongside the spreadsheet as a separate sheet, and then print the chart (Exam requirement).

Create a chart showing the students' average total marks using the marksheet spreadsheet by doing the following steps:

• Select the Students range A1–A11; while holding down the Ctrl key, select the Average Total Mark range K1–K11; after doing so, click the Insert menu and follow the directions as displayed below:

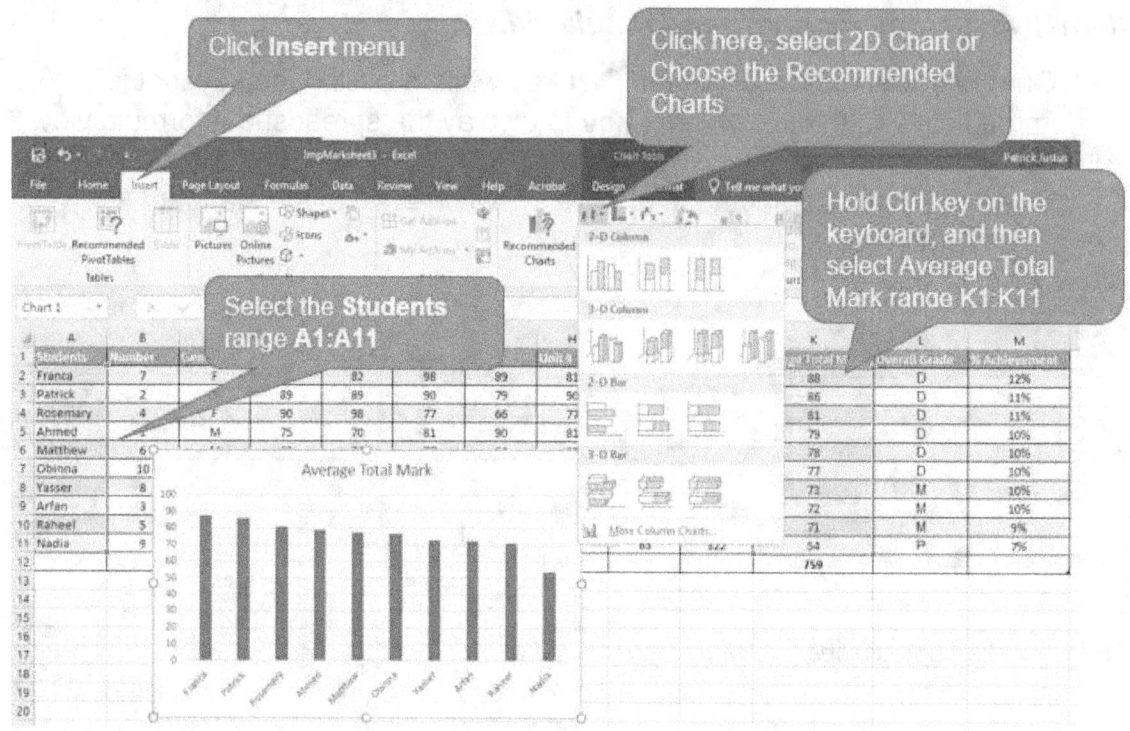

Fig. 20: Generating a Chart from the Spreadsheet – following processes

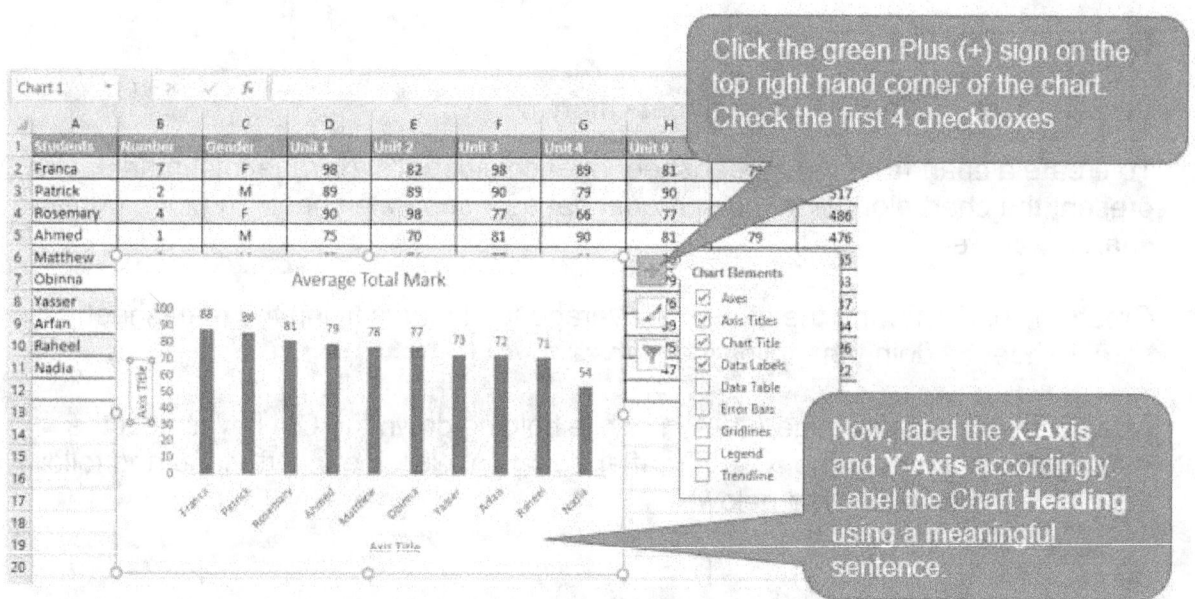

Fig. 21: Generating a Chart from the Spreadsheet – labelling chart headings, axis

Moving Chart to a separate sheet:

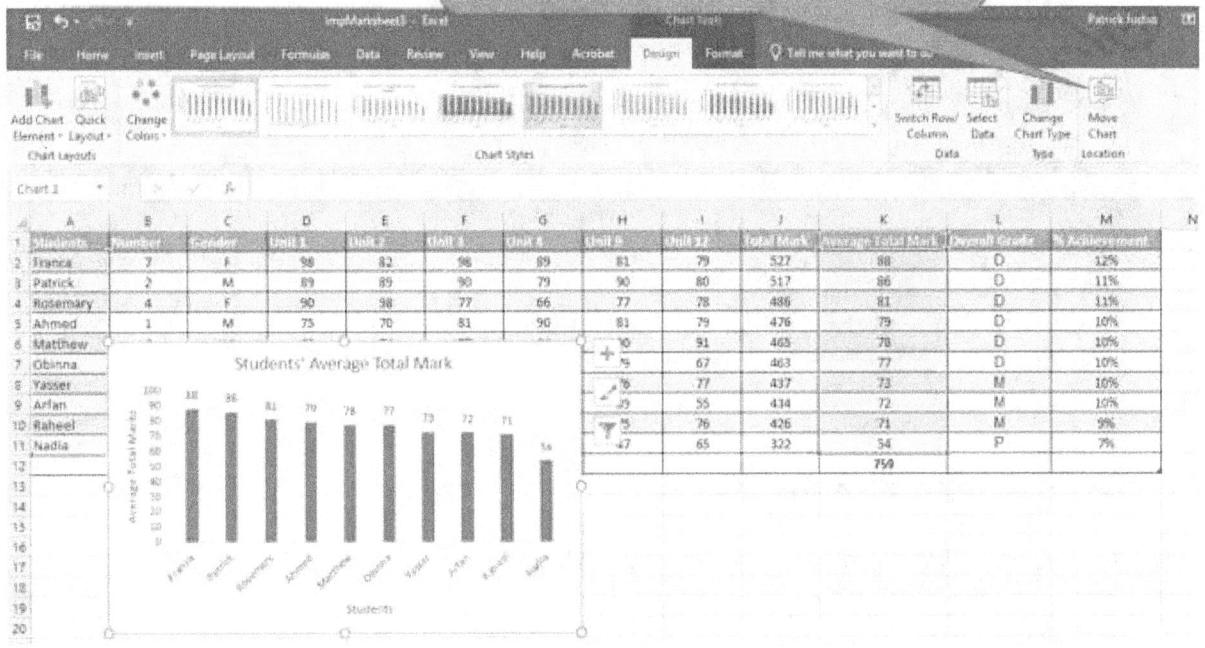

Alternatively, Move Chart to a separate new sheet like so:

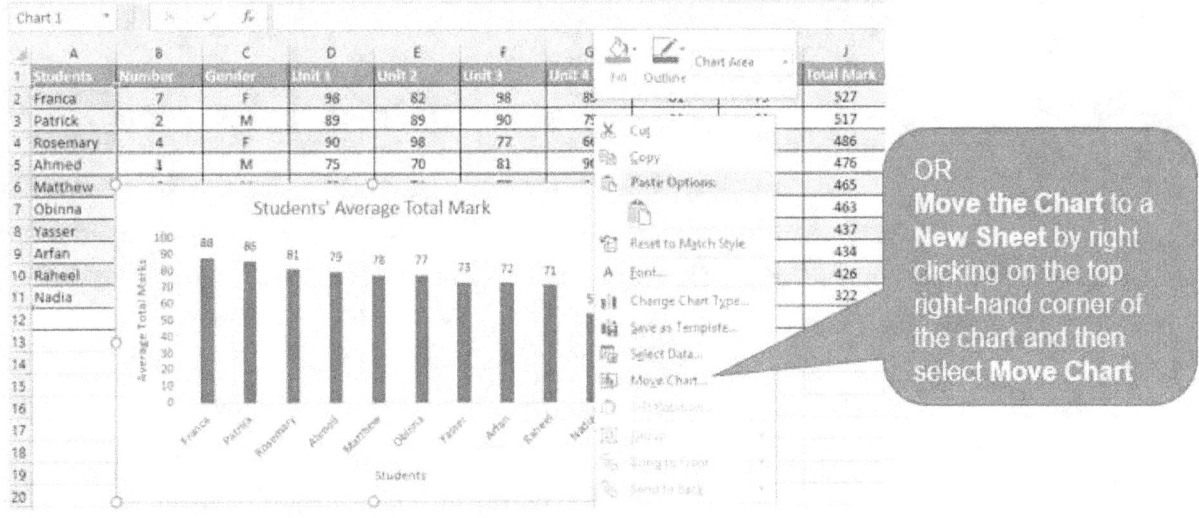

- When either of the above procedures is completed correctly, the **Move Chart** dialogue box appears as follows:

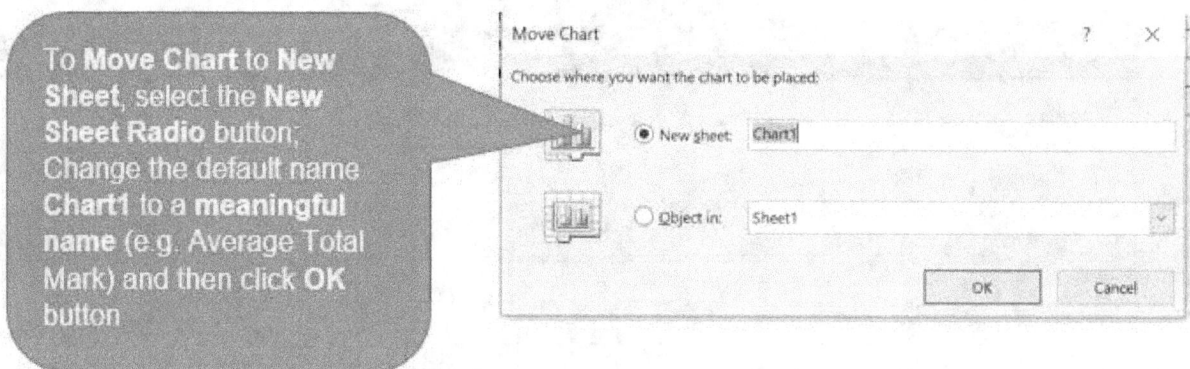

To **Move Chart** to **New Sheet**, select the **New Sheet Radio** button; Change the default name **Chart1** to a **meaningful name** (e.g. Average Total Mark) and then click **OK** button

Chart on same spreadsheet

Chart placed beside the spreadsheet on same sheet

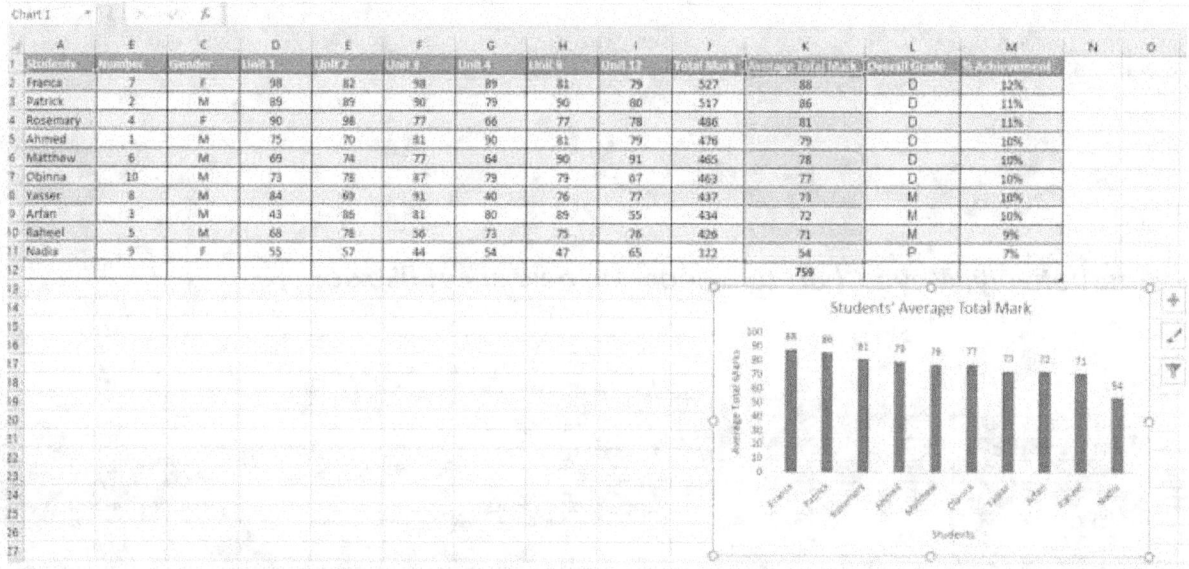

Fig. 22: Chart placed beside the spreadsheet on same sheet

Chart generated and moved onto a separate sheet, then click OK button.

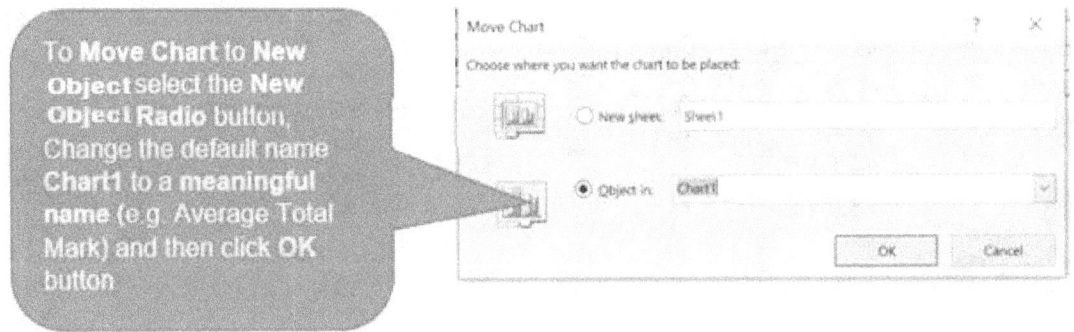

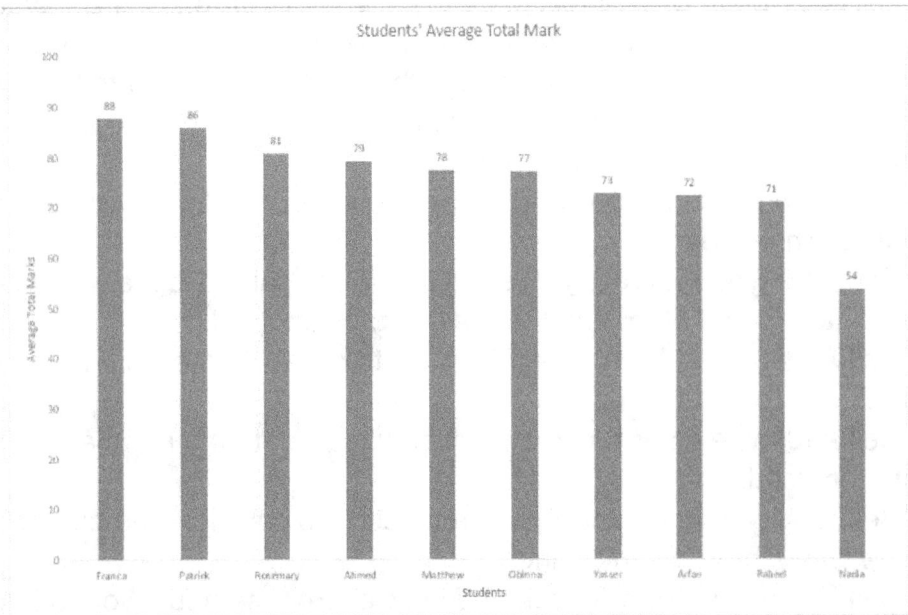

Fig. 23: Chart generated and moved onto a separate sheet

Consolidation

The adage "practise makes perfect" applies here, so use the activities listed below to actively practise applying the spreadsheet modelling techniques you learned today.

Practice Activity

Harlow town's temperature (in degrees Celsius) was recorded over a seven-day period at exactly 09:30 a.m. and the following results recorded:

Day of week	Temp.	Rain	Rounded Temp.
Sunday	+5.0	0	
Monday	-2.6	0	
Tuesday	-3.0	0	
Wednesday	-1.3	0	
Thursday	+3.0	1	
Friday	+4.0	1	
Saturday	+3.5	1	

Tasks:

1. Launch a new spreadsheet; locate cell A1, type in the title: **'Temperature-Rain Recorder'**
2. In cell A3, type in **Day of week**; Cell B3, type in **Temp.**; Cell C3, type in **'Rain'** and in Cell D3, type in **'Rounded Temp'**.
3. In cells A4 to A10, type in the days of the week; in Cells B4 to B10 type in respectively the temperature recorded.
4. Format the spreadsheet as appropriate.
5. For the column titled **Rounded Temp.**; round up the temperature to the nearest whole degree.
6. In Cell A11, type in **Average**; use a function to calculate the average of the raw data and that of rounded temp. (**hint:** Round(cell,0)
7. In Cell A12, type in **Sum**; use a function to calculate the Sum of the raw data and that of rounded temp.
8. In Cell A13, type **Count**; use a function to calculate the number of Temp. data recorded.
9. In Cell A14, type in **Count IF**, use a function to calculate the number of Rain in the week (**hint:** Countif(range,1)
10. In Cell E3, type in **Rain Status**, then in Cell E4, use a function to fetch in the word **'Rained'** when the content in Cell C4 is '1' otherwise the word **'NoRain'** is fetched in – then replicate the formula down into Cell E10.
11. Generate a **chart** to show the rounded temperature for each day of the week.
12. Print (or take a **screenshot**) of the raw spreadsheet and chart on the same sheet.
13. Print (or take a **screenshot**) of the **Formula view** of the completed spreadsheet.

Solution/Outcome

When you correctly complete the 13 activities listed above, your screenshot should appear as follows:

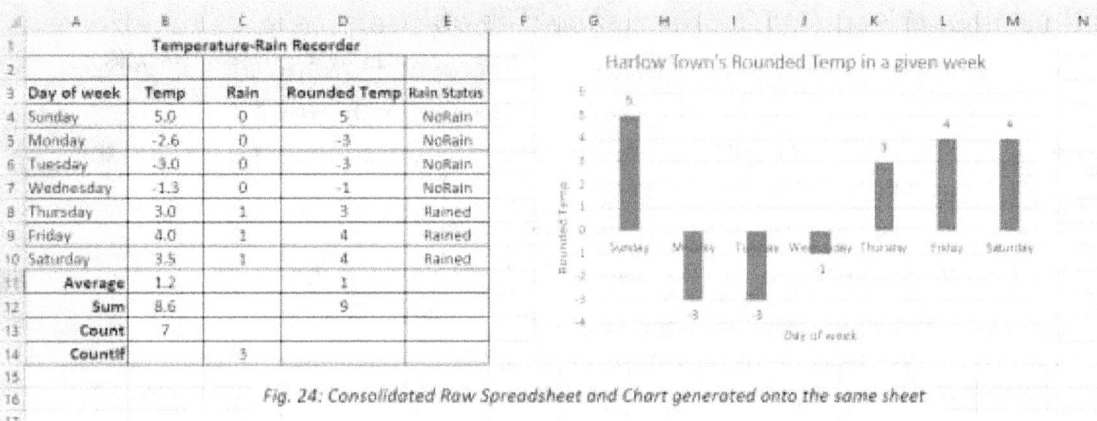

Fig. 24: Consolidated Raw Spreadsheet and Chart generated onto the same sheet

Formula View:

	A	B	C	D	E
1			Temperature-Rain Recorder		
2					
3	Day of week	Temp	Rain	Rounded Temp	Rain Status
4	Sunday	5	0	=ROUND(B4,0)	=IF(C4=1,"Rained","NoRain")
5	Monday	-2.6	0	=ROUND(B5,0)	=IF(C5=1,"Rained","NoRain")
6	Tuesday	-3	0	=ROUND(B6,0)	=IF(C6=1,"Rained","NoRain")
7	Wednesday	-1.3	0	=ROUND(B7,0)	=IF(C7=1,"Rained","NoRain")
8	Thursday	3	1	=ROUND(B8,0)	=IF(C8=1,"Rained","NoRain")
9	Friday	4	1	=ROUND(B9,0)	=IF(C9=1,"Rained","NoRain")
10	Saturday	3.5	1	=ROUND(B10,0)	=IF(C10=1,"Rained","NoRain")
11	Average	=AVERAGE(B4:B10)		=AVERAGE(D4:D10)	
12	Sum	=SUM(B4:B10)		=SUM(D4:D10)	
13	Count	=COUNT(B4:B10)			
14	CountIf		=COUNTIF(C4:C10,1)		
15			Fig 25 - Formula view of the Temperature-Rain Recorder		

PRESENTATION APPLICATION SOFTWARE

Learning outcomes

By the end of this session, learners should be able to:

- Launch a presentation software e.g. Microsoft PowerPoint software
- Identify PowerPoint interface and parts of the work area
- Create a new presentation, enter data, edit data, navigate around the presentation slides
- Insert presentation slides, slide types, slide layout
- Format presentation: bold, italics, font, font size, alignment
- Insert images, table and charts, sound, video, hyperlinks
- Insert footer notes and/or page numbers in all slides
- Add animation and transition effects
- Save, View, Open existing presentations and Print slides as handouts

What is Microsoft PowerPoint?

As a component of its Office tools, Microsoft created the powerful slideshow presentation programme known as PowerPoint. With the use of text, photos, videos, animation, and transitional effects, the programme, which is very well-liked, makes it simple to generate and display facts and information to an audience, such as pupils in a classroom.

Basic PowerPoint presentation creation, editing, viewing, saving, and printing, as well as the addition of tables, charts, animation, and transition effects to presentations, are among the common topics that will be addressed in this session.

Launching Microsoft PowerPoint

Do one of these three things to start Microsoft PowerPoint from Windows 10:

- If there is a PowerPoint icon in the system tray, click it.
- If there is a Microsoft PowerPoint shortcut on the desktop, double-click it.
- Select Microsoft PowerPoint from the Start menu, as shown in the illustration below:

Creating a New Presentation

- This session's examples make use of Microsoft PowerPoint 2016; after starting the presentation, you'll see the interface or dialogue box below.
- A list of template categories will appear on the right once you select the New icon in the left column. Select your preferred template theme or style by clicking it.

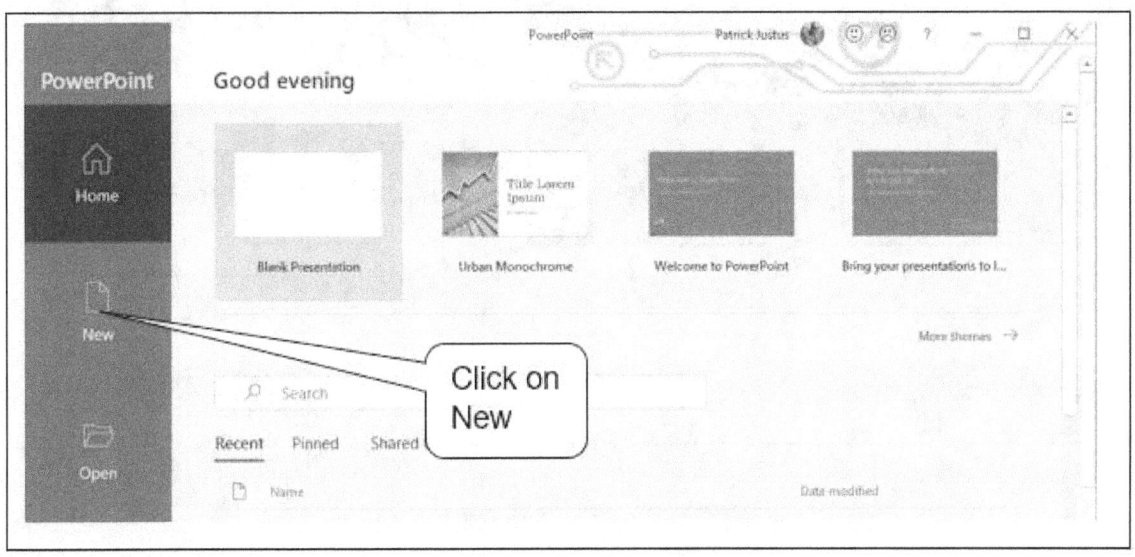

- Select the desired colour theme from the new interface or dialogue box that appears.

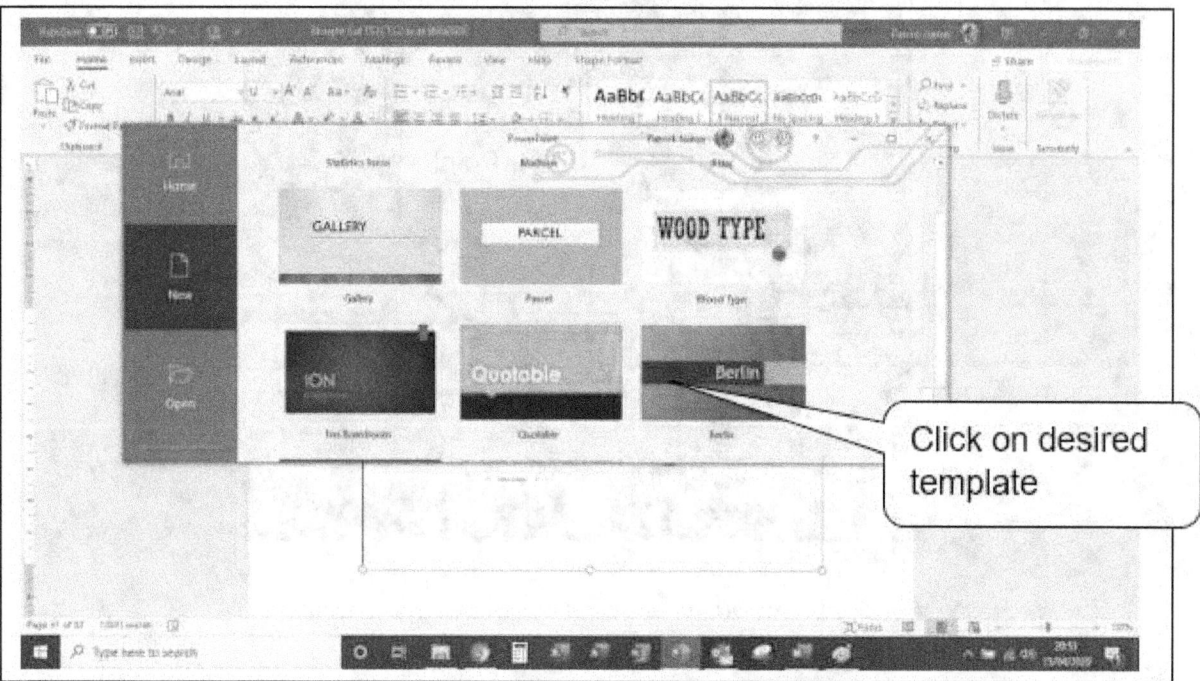

Click on desired template

- A new template schematic will appear; choose your preferred colour scheme and shade by clicking the CREATE button.

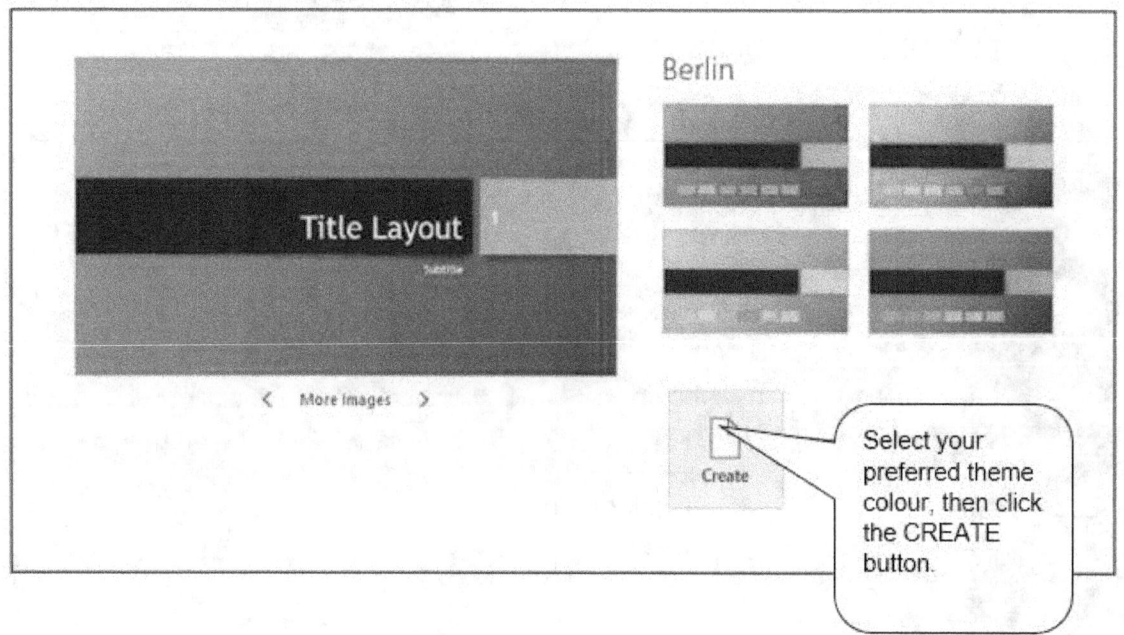

Select your preferred theme colour, then click the CREATE button.

PowerPoint Work Area

Upon a successful start of Microsoft PowerPoint and selection of colour schematics, the following interface will appear:

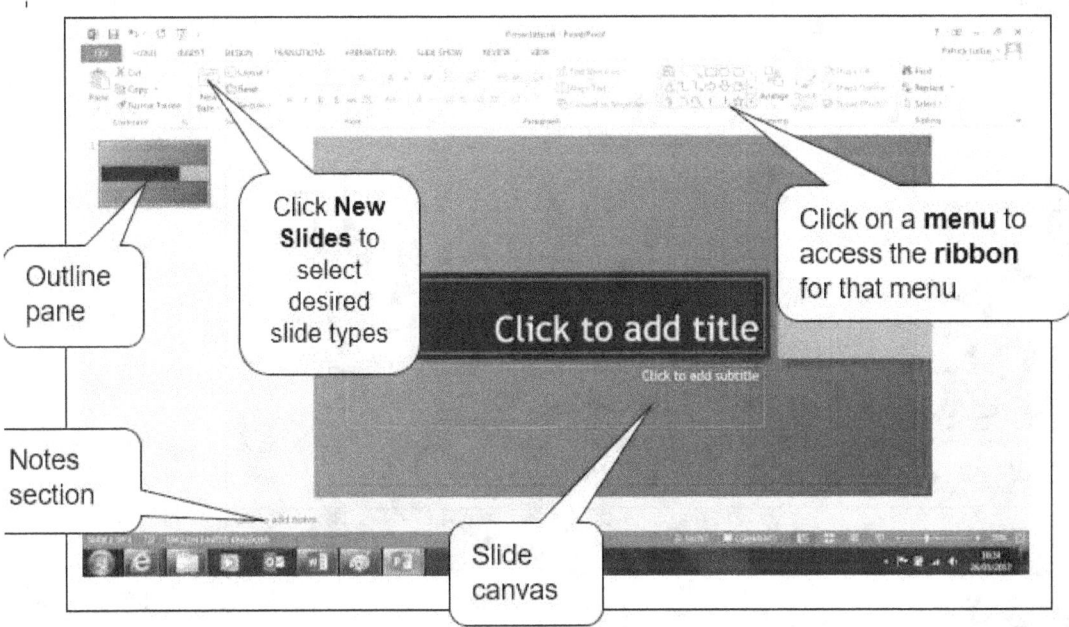

- **Slide canvas** is the primary slide work area in the centre and is used for editing text, images, and content depending on the type of slide being utilised.

- The **outline pane** makes it simple to navigate the presentation slides.

- Below each slide is a section titled "**Notes**." Below each slide, you may add notes or more comprehensive text to provide instructions or hints about what is on each presentation.

- In graphical user interface (GUI) application software, **menus and ribbons** are command tool bars and icons that enable the completion of a variety of activities and tasks. Ribbons have tabs, groups, and commands on them.

Navigating a Presentation

The title slide of a PowerPoint presentation is typically where the presentation begins. By selecting the New Slide icon located under the Home | Slides Ribbon, additional slides can be added to the presentation. By clicking on the tiny picklist arrow on the New Slide icon, you can choose particular slide kinds. Select the slide type you want by navigating to it and clicking.

Viewing particular slides

By selecting individual slides in your presentation's Outline Pane, using the vertical scroll bar or, if available, mouse scroll, you may effortlessly browse among your slides. Slides show up in the centre of the work area or canvas when they are selected.

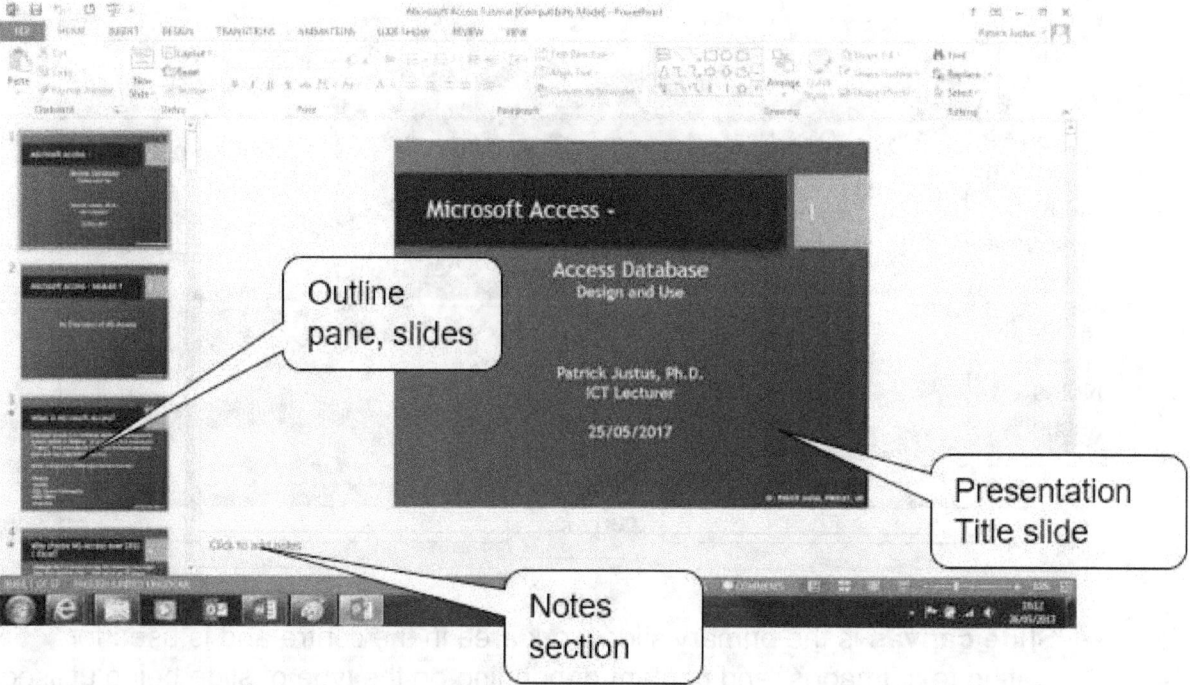

- Depending on the slide type chosen, the following is an example of a 3-section slide:

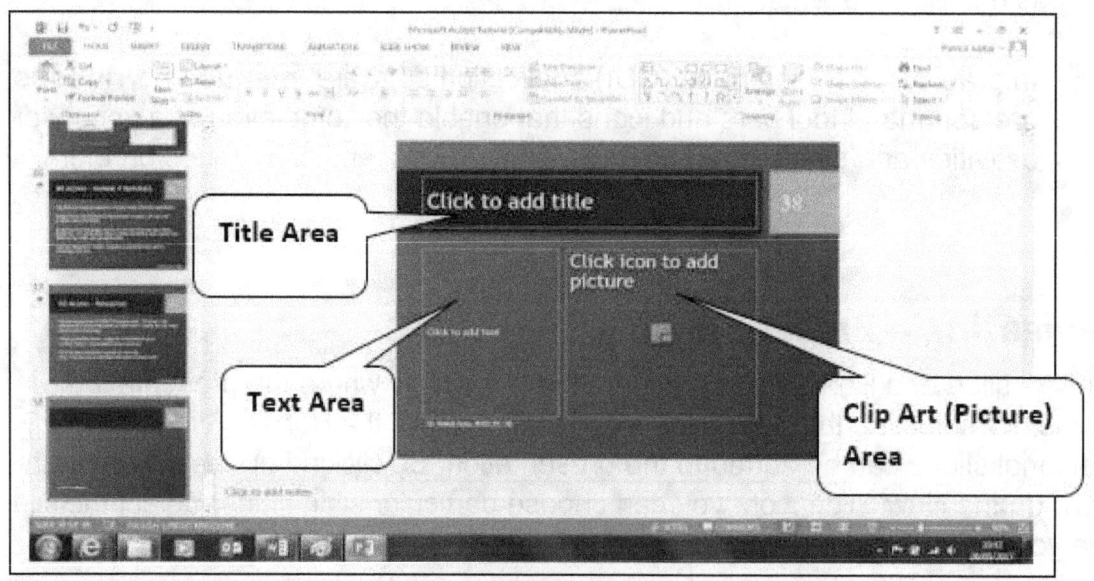

Utilising Elements: Clip Art and Text (Image, Picture)

The essential slide components for making a presentation look professional are text boxes and photos. You can make your own presentation by changing the text and/or adding, editing, and/or replacing the images and texts in the templates, which give you the fundamental design elements for the slides.

Adding and editing text

- To activate the slide's text box, click on it.
- Start entering your text or, if it has already been created elsewhere, cut and paste it.
- Just like in word processing, you can utilise lists with bullets or numbers and alter their types and flows as necessary.

Adding or changing images, pictures

- Where applicable, click the insert icon section of the slide to add, insert, or change photos or pictures.
- You can move photographs to the appropriate area on the slide by resizing, rotating, or scaling them using the picture handles.
- You can insert pictures from a specified file location.
- You can also cut, copy, and paste pictures from files or other apps.

Utilising Tables, Charts, Videos, and Hyperlinks

The other fundamental slide components that are required for boosting a presentation's professional appearance include tables, charts, videos, and hyperlinks.

Although the templates give you simple directions with fundamental design elements for the slides, you will still need to adjust the elements to fit the contents and presentation style that you want.

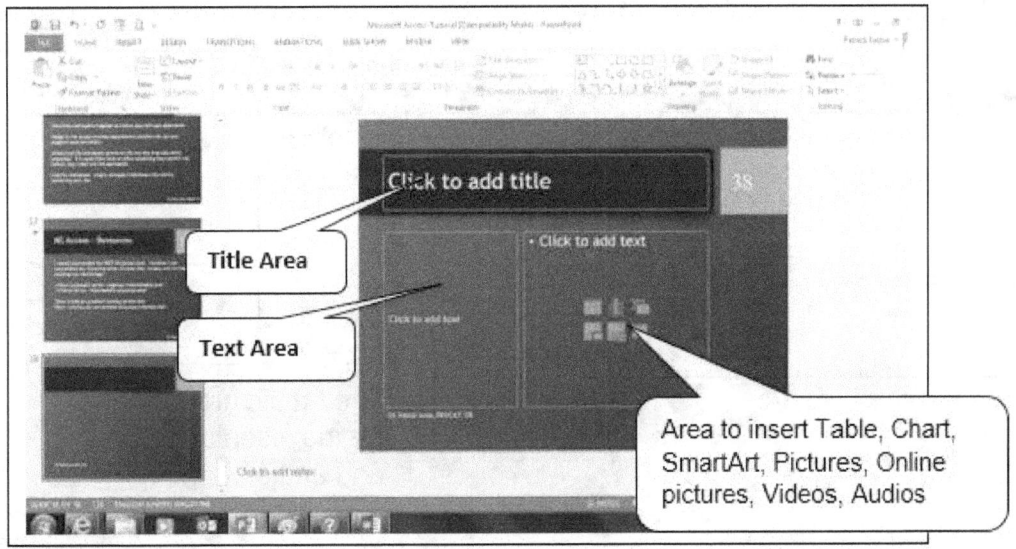

To Add a Table

- A table can be added by clicking the Insert menu and choosing the Table icon from the Tables group of the Insert Ribbon.
- Click the OK button after determining the necessary number of columns and rows for your table.

To Add a Chart

- From the Illustrations group in the Ribbon's Insert menu, click the Chart icon.
- Choose the type of chart you need, and then click OK.

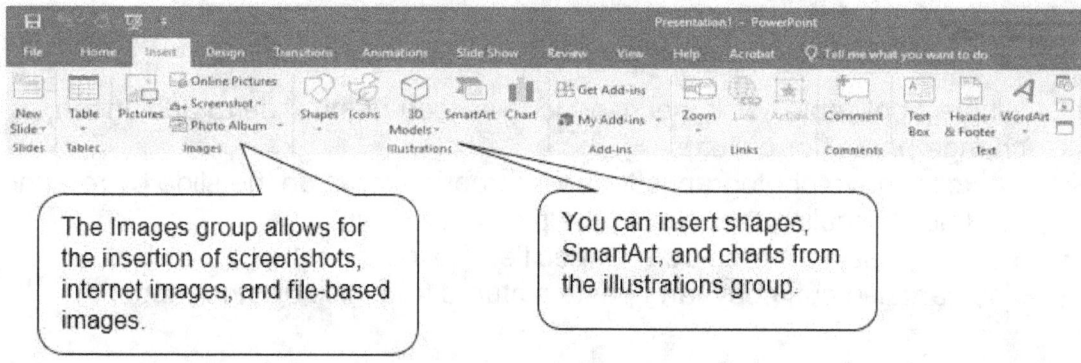

The Images group allows for the insertion of screenshots, internet images, and file-based images.

You can insert shapes, SmartArt, and charts from the illustrations group.

Adding audio and video components

- From the Media group in the Insert Ribbon's Insert Menu, click the Video or Audio symbol.
- Add your video or audio from a computer file, an online source like Youtube.com, or a video embed code (i.e. insert a video embedded code from the web).
- Choose the desired image or photo; adjust the size and positioning as necessary.

The Media group allows for the insertion of video and audio.

Inserting Hyperlinks

- From the Links group in the Insert Ribbon's Insert Menu, click the Link icon.
- Find the desired data as needed and press the OK button.
- You can also insert text or a picture in the usual manner into your slide to make a link, as well as from a web page, such as a YouTube movie.
- Right-click on the text or image after choosing it to establish a link to your document in a file or to a specific webpage online. Additionally, you can utilise hyperlinks to navigate to specific slides or parts of a single document.

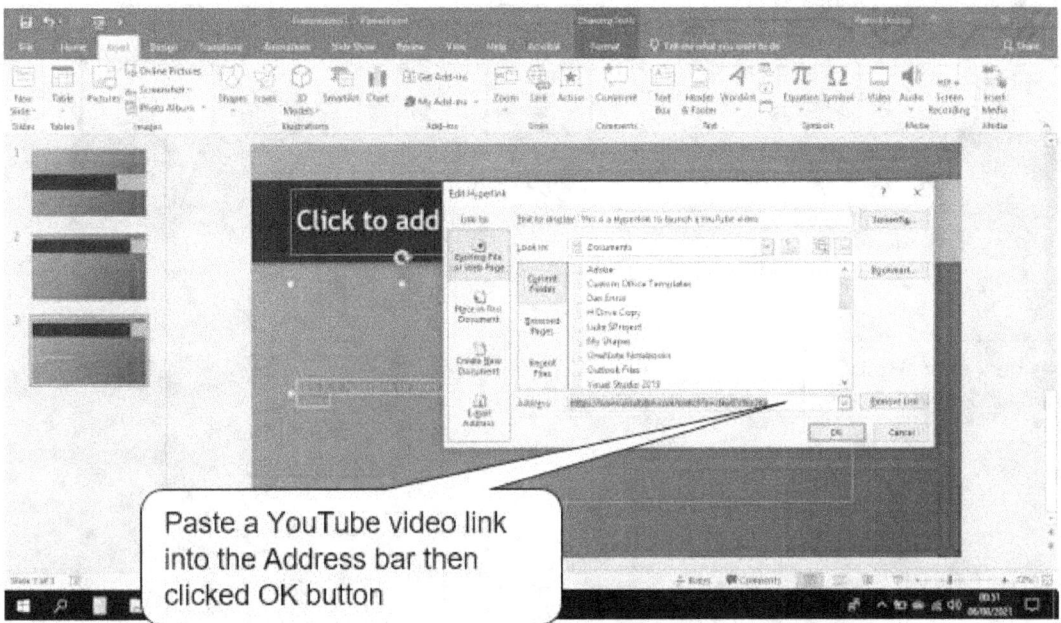

Paste a YouTube video link into the Address bar then clicked OK button

Inserting more Text boxes

- From the Text group of the Insert Ribbon's Text group, click the Text Box icon from the Insert Menu.
- To position a text box on a slide, click and drag it to the correct location before adjusting its size.
- To enter text into the new text box, click on it.
- Another way to start a new text box on a slide is to cut or copy and paste already-written text from another place onto the presentation, then scale it to fit.

Inserting more Shapes, illustrations

- From the Illustrations group of the Insert Ribbon, click the Insert menu and then choose one of the Shapes, SmartArt, or 3D Models icons.
- Carefully follow the relevant procedures.
- For SmartArt visuals, carefully follow the visual cues before clicking the OK button.
- Click, drag, and resize the form, picture, or illustration on your slide as needed.

Formatting PowerPoint Text

- To format text, first choose the relevant text, and then make the necessary changes.
- A text is formatted when one or more of the following are applied to it: bold, italic, underlining, cross through, superscript, subscript, different font types, different font colours, different font sizes, capitalization, text shadow, different text spacing, etc.

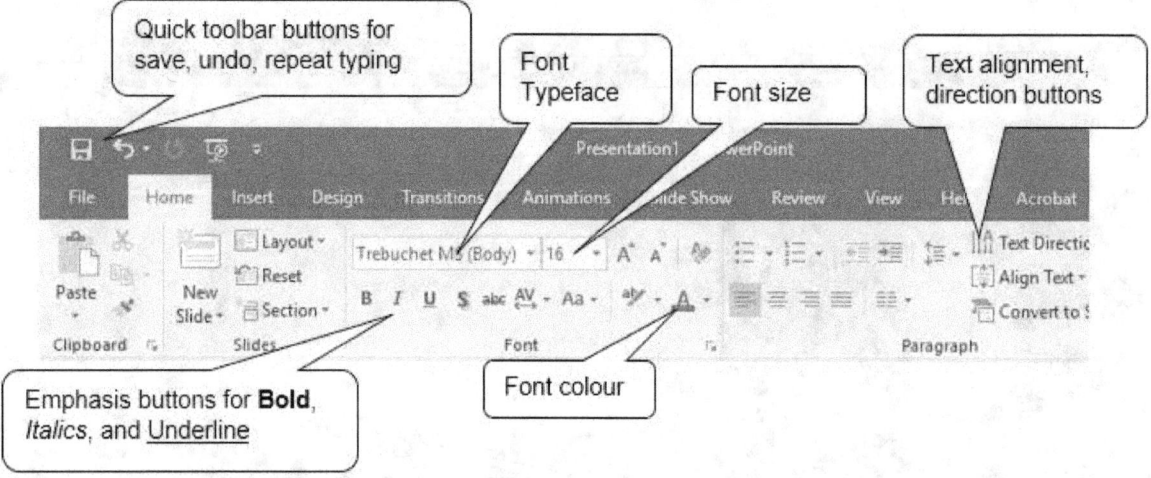

Formatting text

- To format a text box's entire contents at once, click on the border line that appears around the text box and then apply the necessary formatting to it.
- Click on the Home Menu to reveal the Font and Paragraph groups of the Home Ribbon.
- Select a specific text or texts and then apply the necessary formatting to it.
- The Spell checker button is quite helpful and used for editing and removing spelling errors. The Undo button (or Ctrl+Z keys) is used for correcting or modifying unintended mistakes.

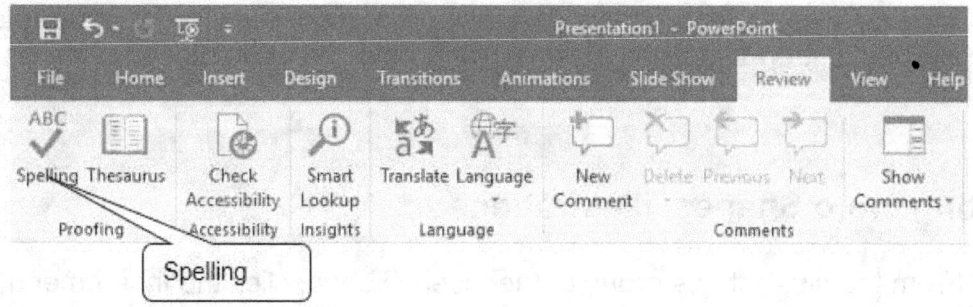

Using the Spell check

- From the Review menu Ribbon, select the Spelling symbol under the Proofing category. The spelling interface section can also be accessed using the keyboard's F7 key.

Consolidation

Preparation Activity

An offline (or reinforced) spreadsheet preparation activity is required for this PowerPoint presentation section in order to produce the data necessary to update a presentation.

Task 1: Determine the kinds of information needed for the presentation.

- You must locate hotel accommodations for a class group.
- When conducting online research, use search engines.

Task 2: Utilising layouts appropriate for the type of information, enter text and other data.

- Create cost information for at least three hotels using spreadsheet software.
- Produce tables and graphs for the presentation.

Spreadsheet Activity Needed:
a) Perform research on three hotels near Alton Tower.
b) Create the spreadsheet displayed below.
c) Use the proper formatting.
d) Determine the total cost in cell B12; copy the formula into cells C12 and D12
e) Create the necessary charts.
f) If everything went according to plan, your spreadsheet should look like this:

The generated table and chart below display the nightly hotel room rates for 11 guests for the presentation:

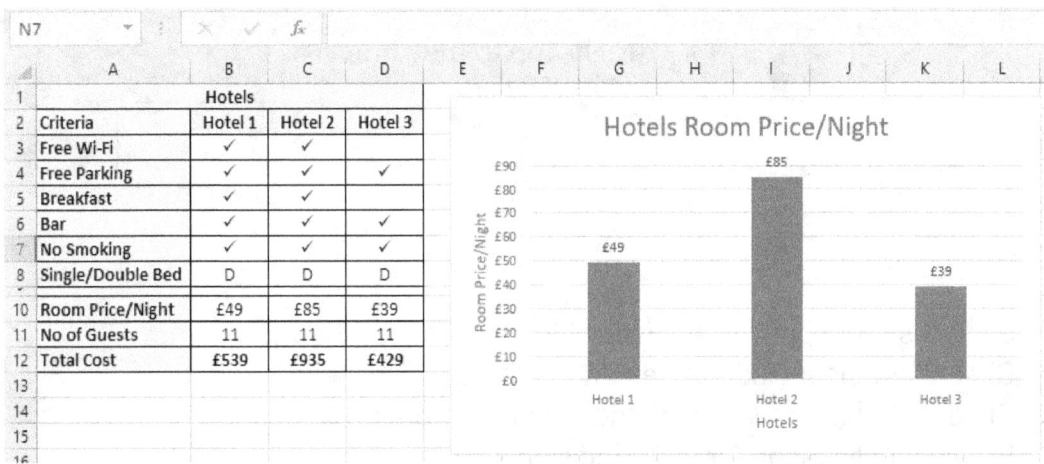

Below is a created table and chart for the presentation that displays the cost of a hotel room per night for 11 students:

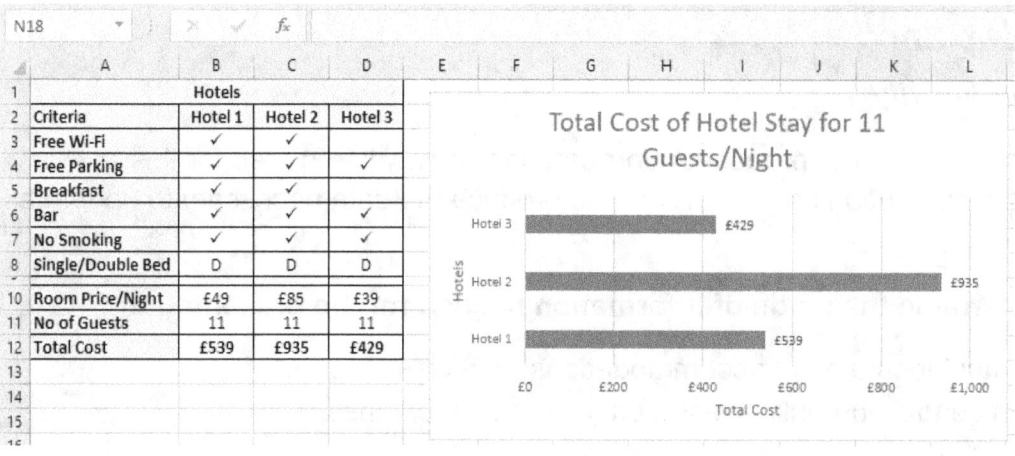

The Presentation Activity

Task 3 – Insert tables and charts in the presentation software

Activity steps required:

1. Open a new PowerPoint presentation and adhere to the following infographics:
2. The title of the presentation, "1-Night Trip to the Alton Towers," should appear on slide 1.

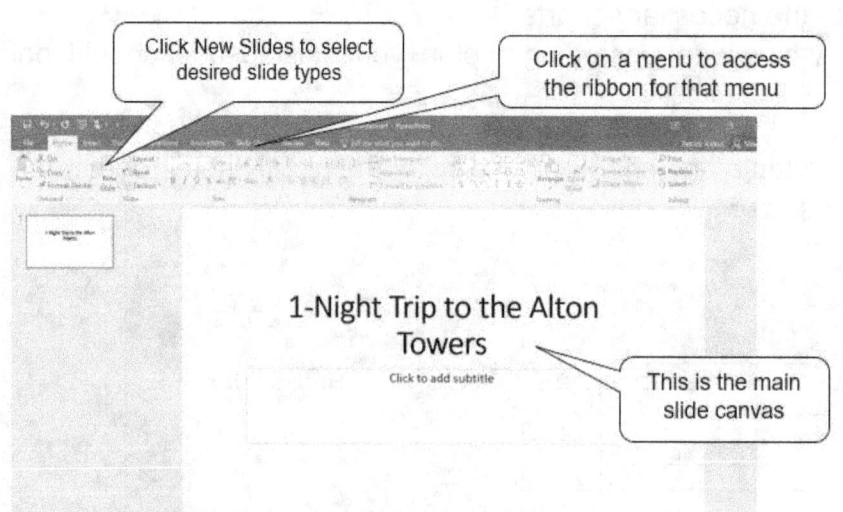

3. Slide 2 should provide a succinct justification for the trip.
4. Slide 3 should include tables and a chart.
5. Slide 4 should recommend one (1) of the hotels.
6. Provide justification for your decision.
7. Add your name and the title of the presentation as a footer to all slides.
8. Add a design type.
9. Print off or take a snapshot of your work.
10. Put three slides on a page.
11. Save your work.

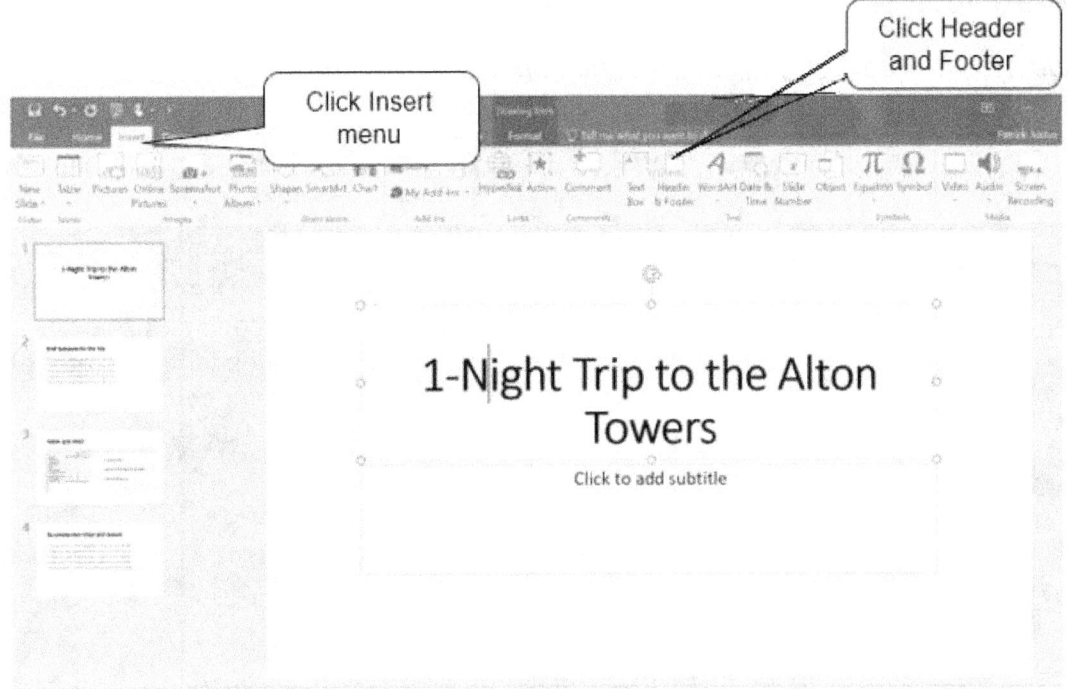

Infographic below shows how to add your name and the title of the presentation as a footer to all slides:

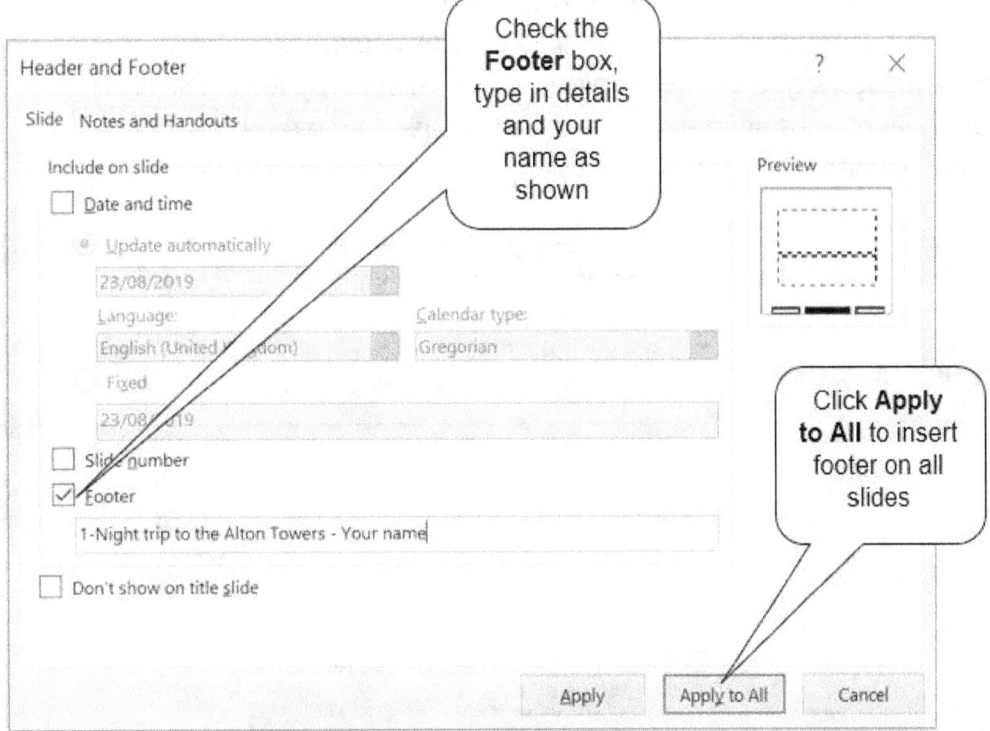

Design Types

Including a design type in your presentation:

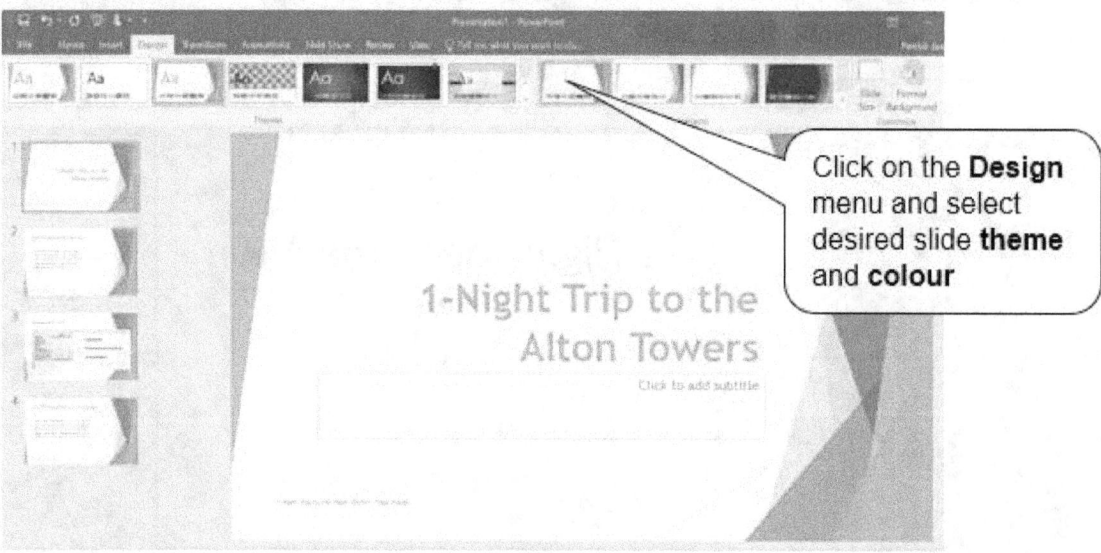

Task 4 – Presentation Effects (Animation)

- Use appropriate animation effects, such as having bullets appear one at a time or visuals fading in, but make sure they are suitable for the audience and the presentation's goals. These might not be necessary for every slide.
- Screenshots of your animation effect can be used as examples.
- Save your efforts.

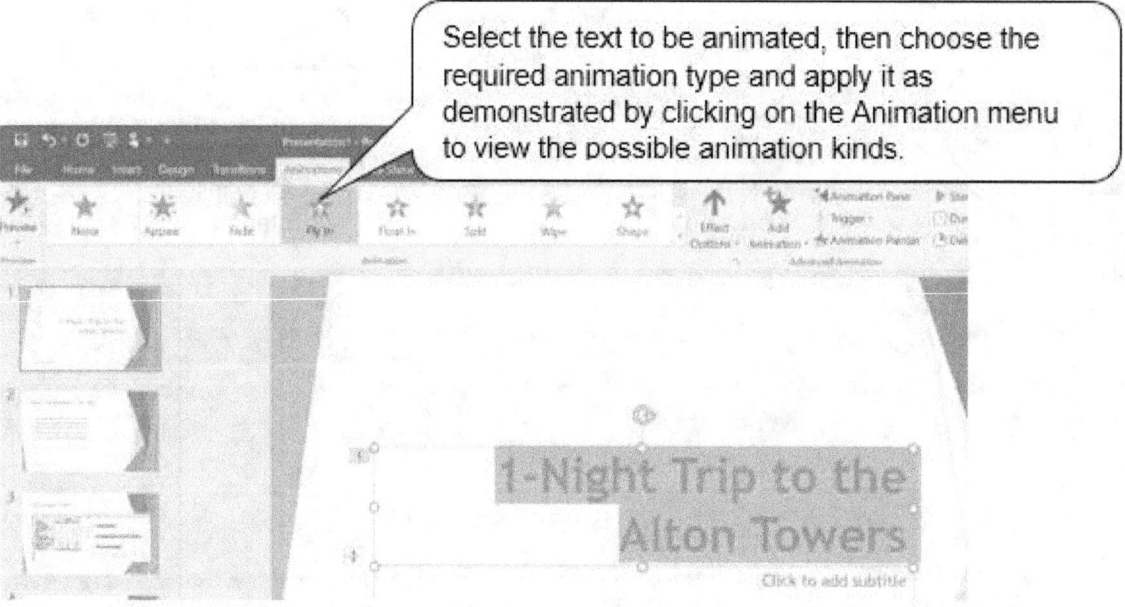

Task 5 – Automatic Slide Transition

- Implement an automated slide transition. The duration of each slide on the screen shouldn't exceed 15 seconds. Add an appropriate transition effect to each slide and an automatic transition to all slides.
- To serve as an example, take screenshots of your transition effect.
- Save your effort.

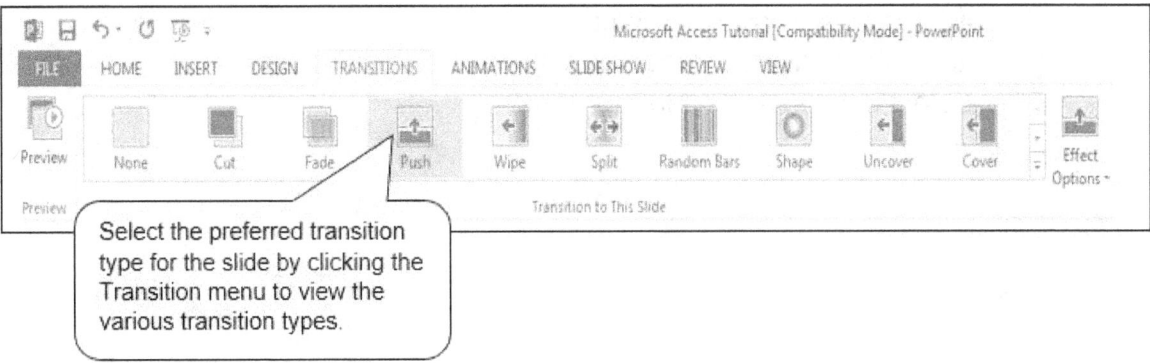

Select the preferred transition type for the slide by clicking the Transition menu to view the various transition types.

Printing a Presentation

Print can be accessed by clicking the File menu option.

- When you select Print, a dialogue window like the one opposite will appear.
- Choose Printer from the drop-down box to choose among available printers (if not the default printer).
- Spin on the number of copies to print, then click the Print button to start printing.

Print Setting Options:
You have five print settings options in PowerPoint:

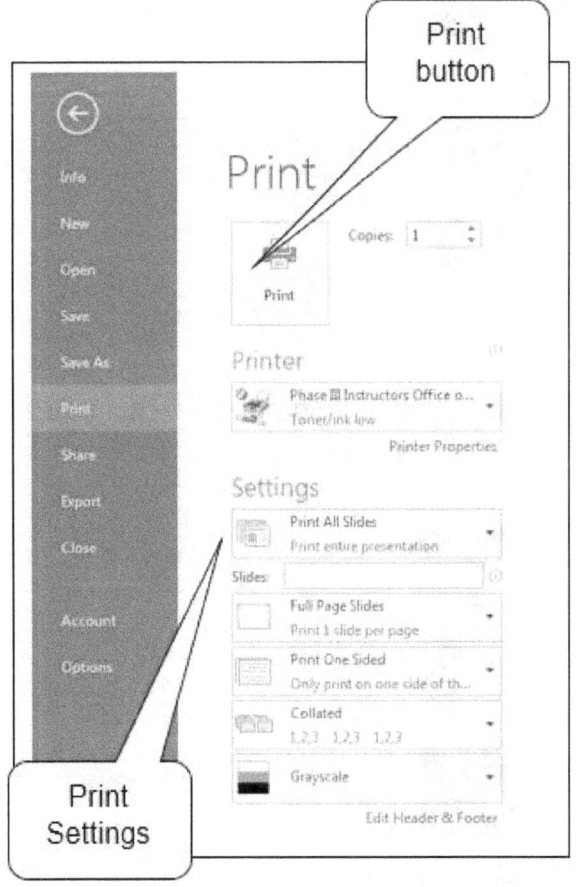

a. Print All Slides to choose the complete presentation or a selection of slides.
b. From the drop-down option, select Full Page Slides, then specify how many slides to print on each page.
c. Collated - printed pages can be either collated or uncollated.
d. Grayscale - choose between colour, grayscale, or black and white prints.
e. Print One Sided - to print only on one side of the paper.

Task 6 – Activity for you to do…

- Put three slides on one page when printing or taking a screenshot of your work:
- To print a slide or slides to a specific number of slides on one page, follow these steps:
    - The image below will appear when you select File | Print from the menu. Then, select Full Page Slides.
    - To see every print layout that is offered, click the tiny picklist on the item labelled, "Full Page Slides"
    - Select 3 slides in one in this case.

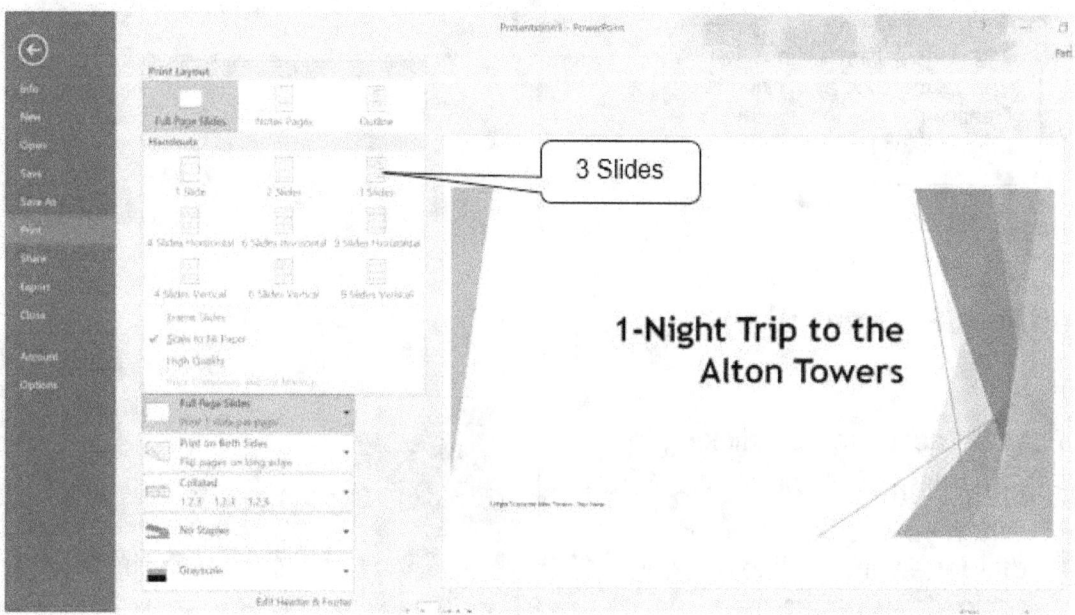

- If carried out correctly, you should see your 3 slides on one page as shown:

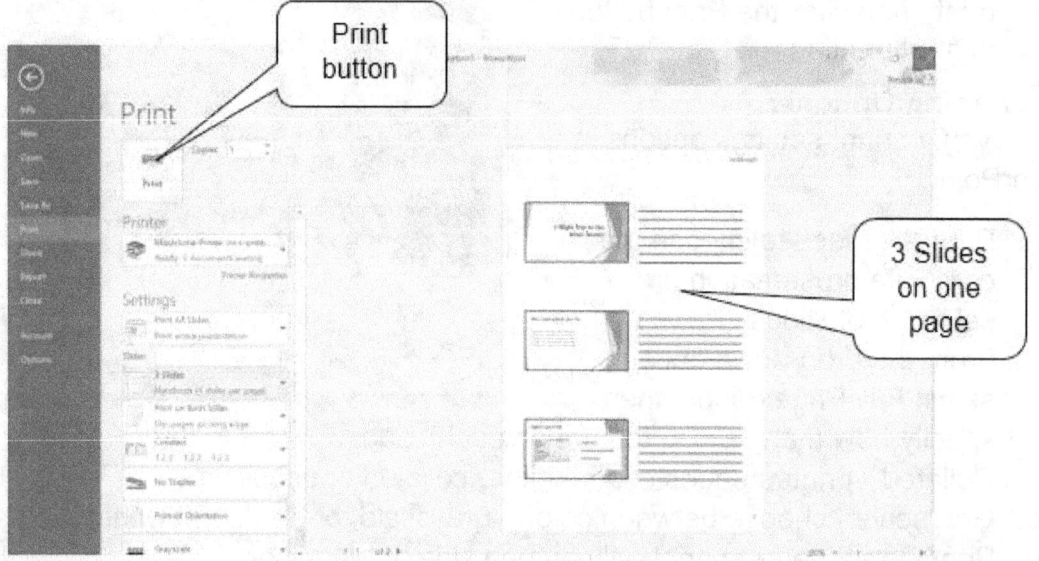

- Take a screenshot or, if you want, click the Print option (by pressing the PrtScr key on your keyboard).
- Paste the image into a Word document and annotate it as instructed.

Viewing a Presentation

To view your presentation:

- Select the 'Slide Show' menu option.
- Select 'From Beginning' in the Start Slide Show group to start the show at the beginning.
- Click 'From Current Slide' to view the slideshow starting with the current slide.
- The keyboard's F5 key can also start a slideshow:

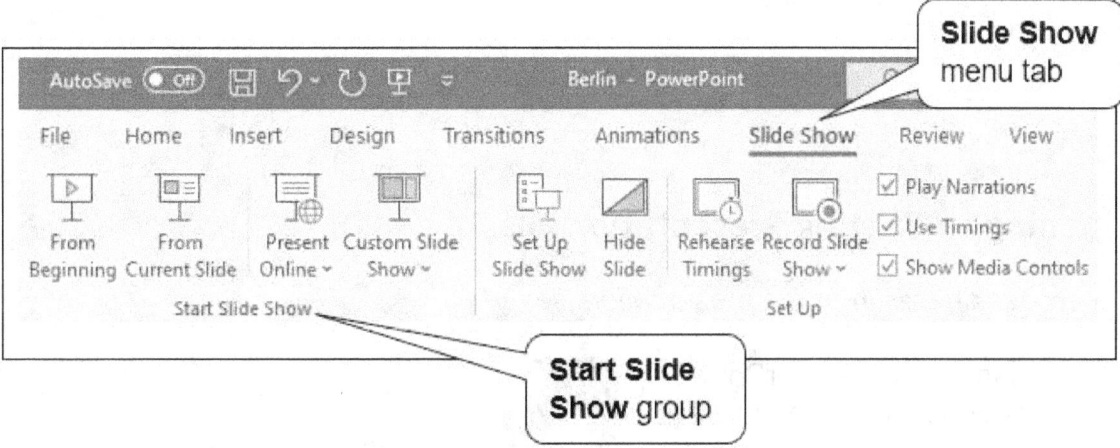

Navigating the slideshow

Using the slideshow's controls:

Any of the following techniques can be used to forward or reverse the slideshows:

- using the directional arrow keys
- clicking the mouse
- pressing the space bar

To end the slideshow presentation

- Simply press the **escape (ESC)** key on the keyboard.

Save and exit a Presentation

To save a slide presentation:

- Select the 'Save As' option under the File menu tab.
- To access quickly and easily, click 'Browse', then 'Save As'; a dialogue box should appear.
- Enter the filename for your presentation in the File name: textbox.
- To select where you want the presentation saved, choose a folder destination.
- Press the 'Save' button.

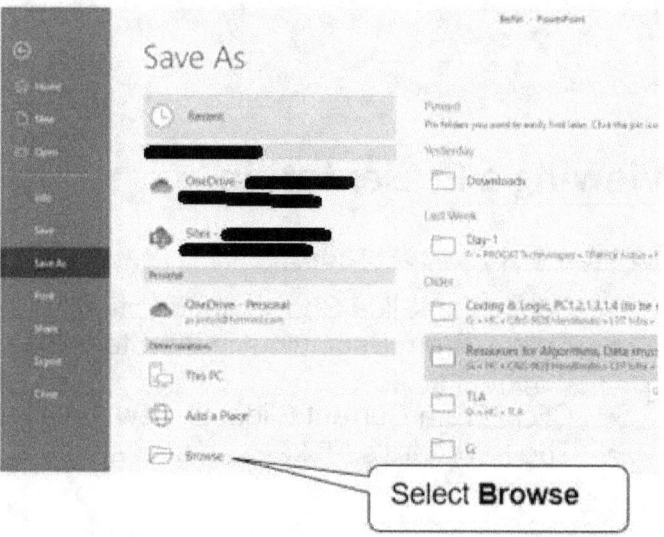

Opening an Existing Presentation File

To access an existing slide presentation file:

- Start or open PowerPoint (or double-click on the file from the file explorer).
- To access your file from PowerPoint programme, select Open from the File menu tab (as shown).
- Click on 'Browse' button to locate the file or folder where your stored file is located and select it.

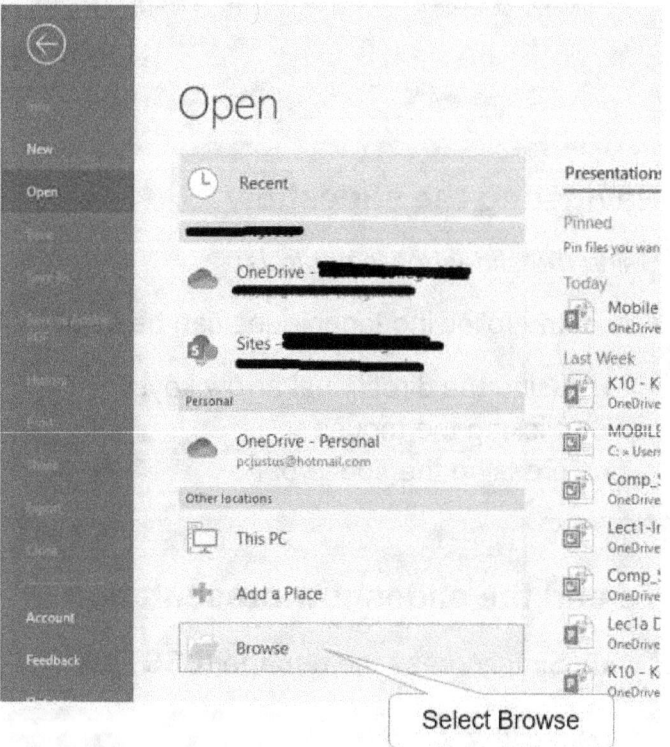

Close/Exit a Presentation

- To shut down and/or close the presentation, click the File menu option.
- Or click the Exit button in the top-right corner of the application to leave the presentation.
- Save the file again if prompted/required.

Consolidation

According to the adage "practise makes perfect," use the PowerPoint skills you have gained today by performing the exercises below to help you actively remember your new knowledge.

- Make a PowerPoint presentation about your favourite sports team, such as the football team. Include bullet point lists with information about the club's history, the players, and their positions on the field, among other things.
- Display their statistics on the league table using a table and a chart.
- Include visual representations of the club's logo and colours.
- Add a footer with your name and the name of the club to each slide.
- Include text effects and transitions in your slides.
- A word of warning before your exams: limit the use of complex graphics to make it simpler to post your finished presentation online.

Lesson 5

FURTHER SPREADSHEET APPLICATIONS

Learning Outcome:
- Recap, improve your knowledge of and competence with spreadsheets.
- Format the spreadsheet to meet your needs.
- Perform basic math operations.
- Adjust the spreadsheet's columns and rows.
- Practice using the IF and IF AND functions.

5. Engineering Data – Height of students
- Using the corresponding spreadsheet cells in Excel, enter the spreadsheet below.

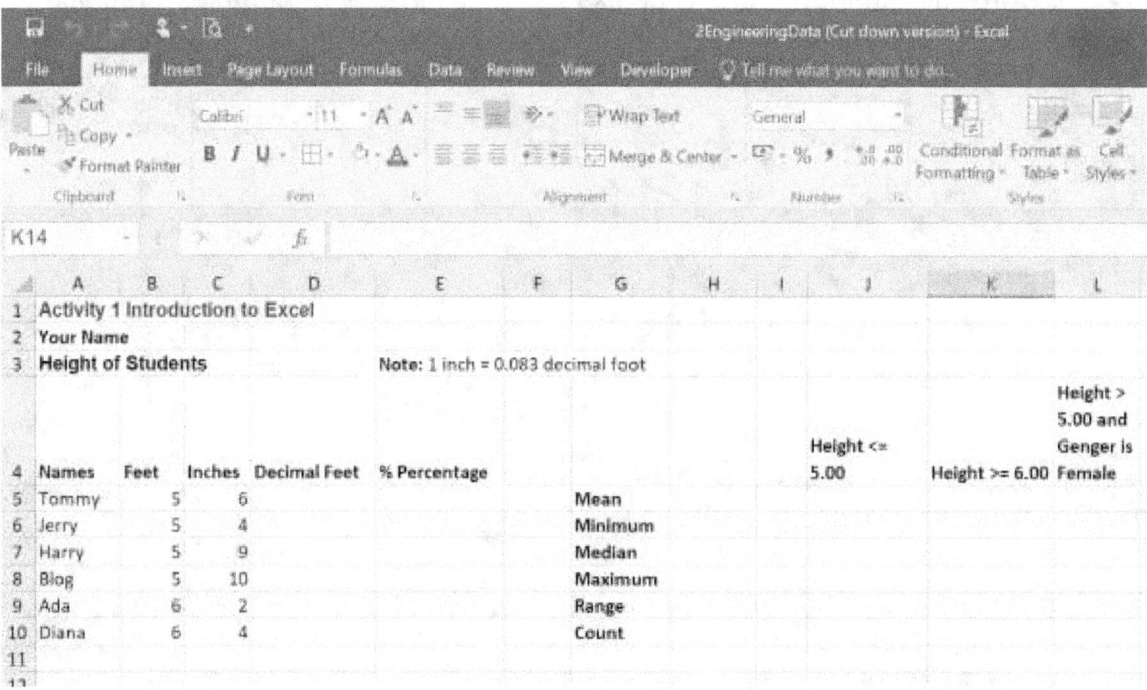

Activity 1:

- Format the spreadsheet according to the specifications in lesson 2
- Modifying the spreadsheet's rows and columns
- Carry out basic mathematical operations as described in lesson 2.
- Delete columns F and I
- The information in cell J4 should be changed to "Height <=6.00"
- The word "genger" should be changed to "gender" in cell L4 because it is incorrect.
- Insert a new column in between Columns A and B.

- Put the term "Gender" in the new cell B4, then type "M" for a male student and "F" for a female student as appropriate.
- If everything went well, your spreadsheet should appear as follows:

	A	B	C	D	E	F	G	H	I	J	K
1	Activity 1 Introduction to Excel										
2	Your Name										
3	Height of Students					Note: 1 inch = 0.083 decimal foot					
4	Names	Gender	Feet	Inches	Decimal Feet	% Percentage Height			Height <= 6.00	Height >= 6.00	Height > 5.00 and Gender is Female
5	Tommy	M	5	6			Mean				
6	Jerry	M	5	4			Minimum				
7	Harry	M	5	9			Median				
8	Blog	M	5	10			Maximum				
9	Ada	F	6	2			Range				
10	Diana	F	6	4			Count				

Activity 2:

- Calculate the **Decimal Feet** column; locate cell E5, type in a formula to calculate the decimal feet (apply the note factor provided in cell F3), and replicate down the column.
- Calculate the **% Percentage Height** column; locate cell F5, type in a formula to calculate the % percentage height (calculate the total decimal feet for all students and then apply absolute cell referencing in your divisor)
- Based on data from the decimal feet, perform all functions/formula in column H for all corresponding quantities in column G (hint – see AutoSum icon below):

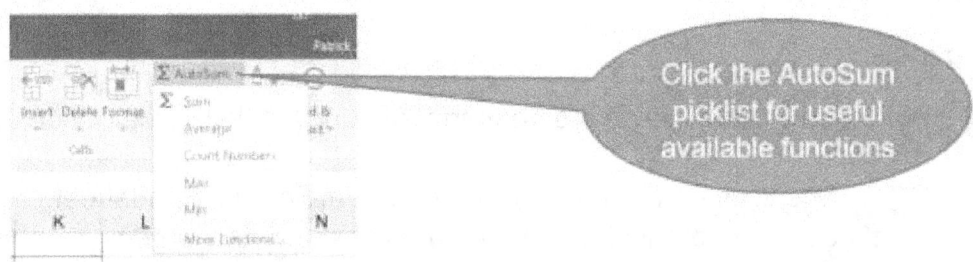

- If carried out correctly, your spreadsheet should now look like this:

	A	B	C	D	E	F	G	H	I	J	K
1	Activity 1 Introduction to Excel										
2	Your Name										
3	Height of Students					Note: 1 inch = 0.083 decimal foot					
4	Names	Gender	Feet	Inches	Decimal Feet	% Percentage Height			Height <= 6.00	Height >= 6.00	Height > 5.00 and Gender is Female
5	Tommy	M	5	6	5.50	16%	Mean	5.82			
6	Jerry	M	5	4	5.33	15%	Minimum	5.33			
7	Harry	M	5	9	5.75	16%	Median	5.79			
8	Blog	M	5	10	5.83	17%	Maximum	6.33			
9	Ada	F	6	2	6.17	18%	Range	1.00			
10	Diana	F	6	4	6.33	18%	Count	6.00			
11				Total:	34.91						
12											

Activity 3:

- Perform further spreadsheet practice using the IF, IF AND functions
- Apply the 'IF' Functions for columns I and J;
- Apply the 'IF AND' functions for column K

Note: Display the respective students' decimal feet heights from column E when the outcome is TRUE and a blank space ("") when the outcome is FALSE.

The Solution - the Finished Spreadsheet

- If you have carried out the above activities correctly, your spreadsheet should now look like this:

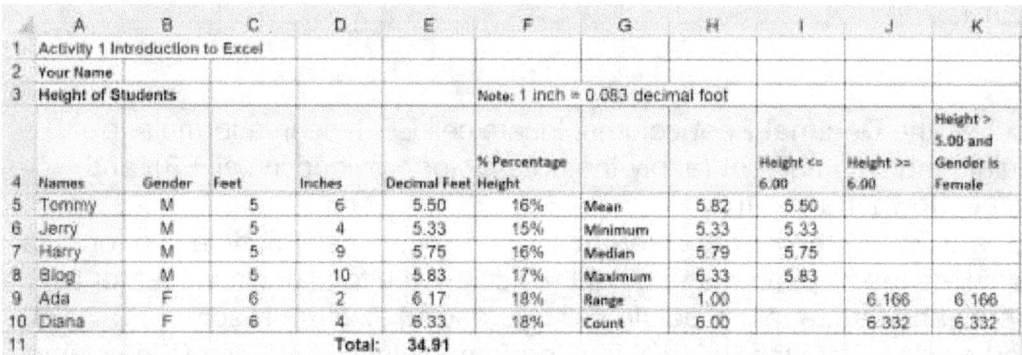

	A	B	C	D	E	F	G	H	I	J	K
1	Activity 1 Introduction to Excel										
2	Your Name										
3	Height of Students					Note: 1 inch = 0.083 decimal foot					
4	Names	Gender	Feet	Inches	Decimal Feet	% Percentage Height			Height <= 6.00	Height >= 6.00	Height > 5.00 and Gender is Female
5	Tommy	M	5	6	5.50	16%	Mean	5.82	5.50		
6	Jerry	M	5	4	5.33	15%	Minimum	5.33	5.33		
7	Harry	M	5	9	5.75	16%	Median	5.79	5.75		
8	Blog	M	5	10	5.83	17%	Maximum	6.33	5.83		
9	Ada	F	6	2	6.17	18%	Range	1.00		6.166	6.166
10	Diana	F	6	4	6.33	18%	Count	6.00		6.332	6.332
11				Total:	34.91						

Consolidation

Using the spreadsheet above:

- For these 3 tasks, paste a screenshot of your results in your evidence Word document:
  a. Showcase a formula view of your completed spreadsheet
  b. Sort the spreadsheet in the order of students' names
  c. Generate a chart of students' decimal height onto the same spreadsheet and as a separate sheet.

DATABASE APPLICATION SOFTWARE

Learning outcomes

- Recognising the database
- Planning and Implementing a Database
- Manipulating the data in the database tables
    - Sorting,
    - querying a database using just one criterion
    - querying a database using several criteria
- Extensive query options
- Create a simple database form
- Create a simple database report
- Import or open a text file into the database

1. INTRODUCTION TO DATABASE SYSTEM

Scenario

You are a Junior IT Support at Mayfair Used Car Company. In your first assignment, you are mandated with the design and implementation of a simple database system, which can hold details of their fleet and will enable users to easily Create (add/append data), Read (search), Update (edit) and Delete records (CRUD) in the system.

The Company's computer platform is based on Microsoft Windows and Microsoft Office Suite.

1.1. MICROSOFT ACCESS COMMANDS AND FUNCTIONS

a. How to use Access **database** for data administration (**to create tables, queries, forms, show a few advanced features**)
b. How to use Access **database** for data manipulation (to add, edit, update data)
c. How to use Access **database** to extract (retrieve data) useful information

The Word and Excel windows are familiar to you if you've used Windows software in the past. Although the Access window differs slightly from the Word and Excel windows, since they are members of the same family of integrated software, you will get more familiar with it as you use it.

This Access tutorial presume that you have some familiarity with the fundamentals of Word processing and likely have some knowledge of Excel spreadsheets.

In this section of the tutorial, we'll build a one-table database, also known as a flat file, and add forms, queries, and reports to examine some of Access' data administration features.

Effective database development and design involve in-depth research and planning. The design and development of a flat-file would be rather simple, straight-forward and easy to grasp. For this reason, only the fourth and fifth item from the following list of database design approach will be examined or explained:

a. Data normalisation is not covered in this book.
b. ER Analysis Schema - not discussed in this book
c. Entity Relationship Diagram (ERD) - not discussed in this book
d. Data Dictionary - not discussed in this book
e. Basic Data analysis and structure (Data Definition)

1.2. PLANNING THE DESIGN

1.2.1. Database Structure

It is best practise to first plan and decide on the type of database you are going to construct, the data table to be formed, the data that will be stored in it, the quantity of the data, the type of data validation that will be implemented, etc. The term "Data definition" is occasionally used to describe this database structure.

Data definition is a source of information about data that provides a description of the data elements (or fields) used in the creation of databases. It makes building the database much simpler. The database structure that will be utilised to build the Mayfair Used Cars database tables is shown in the table below:

Field Name	Data Type	Other Information
Vehicle ID PK	Number	Long Integer **NOT NULL**
MAKE	Text	Field size – 6, Data Validated
TYPE	Text	Field size - 20
DOORS	Text	Field size - 20
COLOUR	Text	Field size - 20
REGISTRATION	Date	Field size – 8 (short date)
PRICE	Currency	Field size - 20

There are certain significant data elements in the database structure above that may need to be defined immediately, but a more thorough explanation can be discovered in advanced database development or by conducting exploratory research:

a. Fields (fieldnames) are the names of the attributes or properties that make up the database object that is currently being developed.

b. Data types - this section explains the types of data that should be kept in each field. The basic data types are text, number, date, and currency. Text refers to any character on the keyboard; number refers to arithmetic numbers or values that we can add together; in this case, this could be a short number or a long number.

c. Primary key (PK), which is often italicised in a database structure and used as an identifier for uniquely identifying a record in the database, is referred to as the unique field. A primary key, or unique identifier, is required for each record in a database.

d. Additional details like field size, NOT NULL, and verified fields (field size refers to the character space that will be allotted in memory for storing data in the database; NOT NULL is a critical phrase used in database design to refer to the primary key, which cannot be left blank). A verified field indicates a regulated field in the database, which facilitates data entry, prevents errors, and supports data integrity. Any new primary key must have a value and cannot be left blank.

1.3.   IMPLEMENTING THE DATABASE

Assumption

It is assumed that ALL students have basic knowledge of Microsoft Windows and may have used Office Word and possibly Excel Spreadsheet.

Part 1 - Create and populate a database

- For this task, you must develop and put into practise database designs utilising the data structure as a starting point. The process of creating the table will be followed by that of populating it with data.
- Tables are used to store data in Microsoft Access. Your data will be tracked in the table you create. Information on a person, thing, or entity is contained in each record in the table (an entity is an object or thing about which we keep information, e.g. a database of cars).

1.4.   Design and Develop the Mayfair Used Car Company Systems

1.4.1. Creating a Database Table

If the Access programme isn't already running, launch it as necessary (this example runs on Windows 10 and utilises Office 2016):

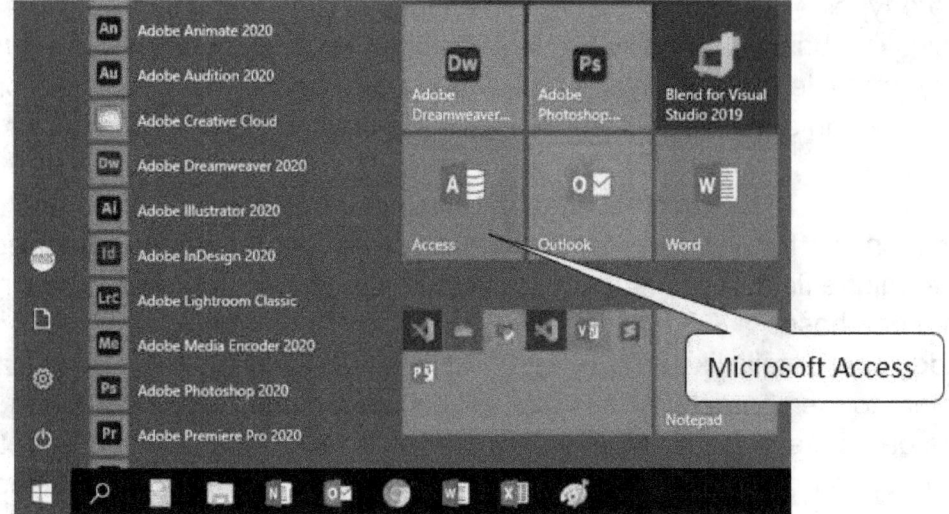

The image above shows a section of Microsoft Windows 10 comprising a variety of software icons on the Start-up interface – locate **Microsoft Access 2016** and click on it with your mouse pointer. When done correctly the Access Database Creation interface should be displayed as shown below – carefully follow the infographics as you progress on the programme:

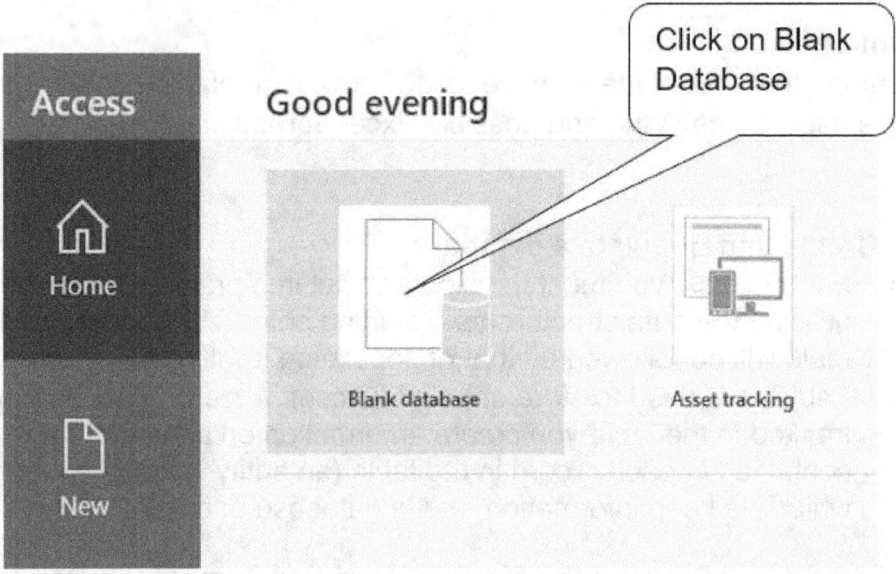

Creating Desktop Database

Clicking on the New **Blank Database** button will display a dialogue box for the database filename creation. At this stage, you should provide a **filename** and **location** for the Access database to be created and saved; click on the **Create** button to launch the saved **Access database Control Panel** from where you can define the database structure:

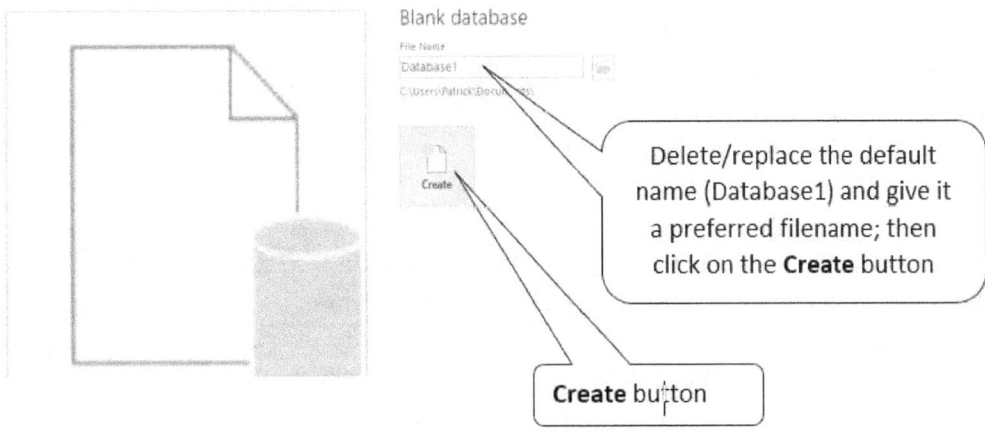

Blank database

File Name

Database1

C:\Users\Patrick\Docu...

Create

Delete/replace the default name (Database1) and give it a preferred filename; then click on the **Create** button

Create button

1.4.2. Defining the Data Structure

When defining the database structure, you might need to switch between Datasheet View and Design view by clicking on the 'View' symbol or icon as shown or by clicking on the small picklist of the File | View to choose the design or Datasheet view from there. If you're prompted to save the default table named Table1, change that to a preferred name, such as Cars:

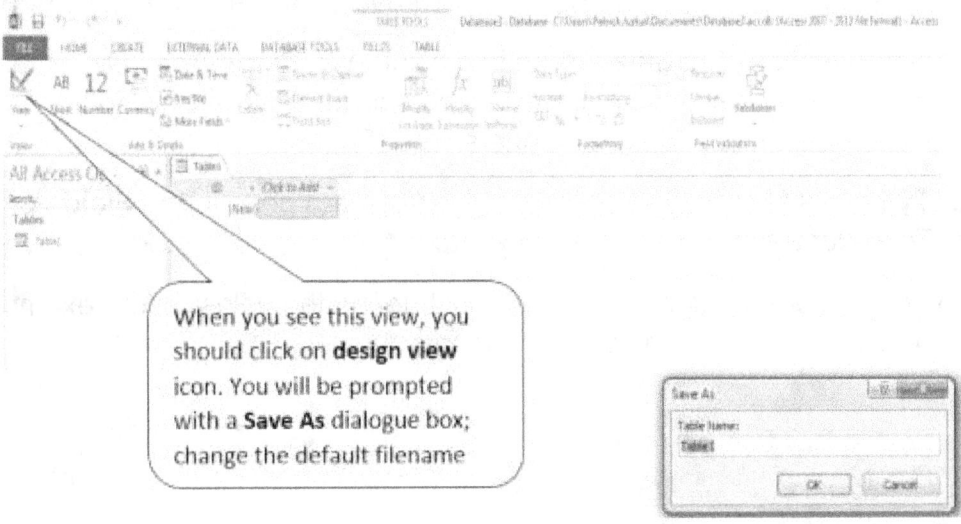

When you see this view, you should click on **design view** icon. You will be prompted with a **Save As** dialogue box; change the default filename

Save As

Table Name:

Table1

OK   Cancel

Next, the following database design view is displayed:

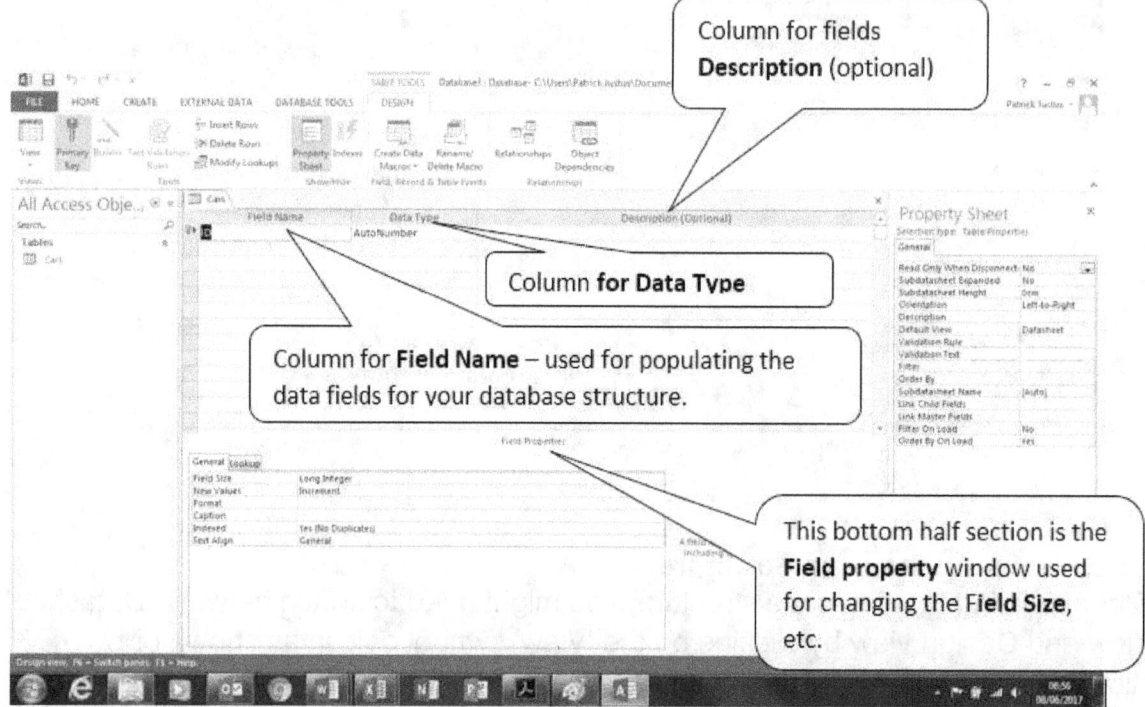

Defining and creating a table consists mainly of the defined fields you wish to have in your database structure. Each part of the record has a **Fieldname** and **Data type**

The **fieldname** identifies the **data** stored in a column. A **fieldname** can contain up to 255 characters including spaces. However, the shorter the **Fieldname** the more likely the whole database is to print on one sheet of paper.

The **Data Type** tells Microsoft Access what kind of **Data** goes in the **Field**, for example, Text, Numbers, Dates, Currency, etc.

Before you can enter the information, you must define the fields. In our example, you will need to define the following fields about cars:

MAKE

TYPE

PRICE

DOORS

COLOUR

REGISTRATION

Thus, you should enter each of the above data fields into the database design menu window one after the other as defined in your database structure – follow the infographics and the instructions given within the callouts:

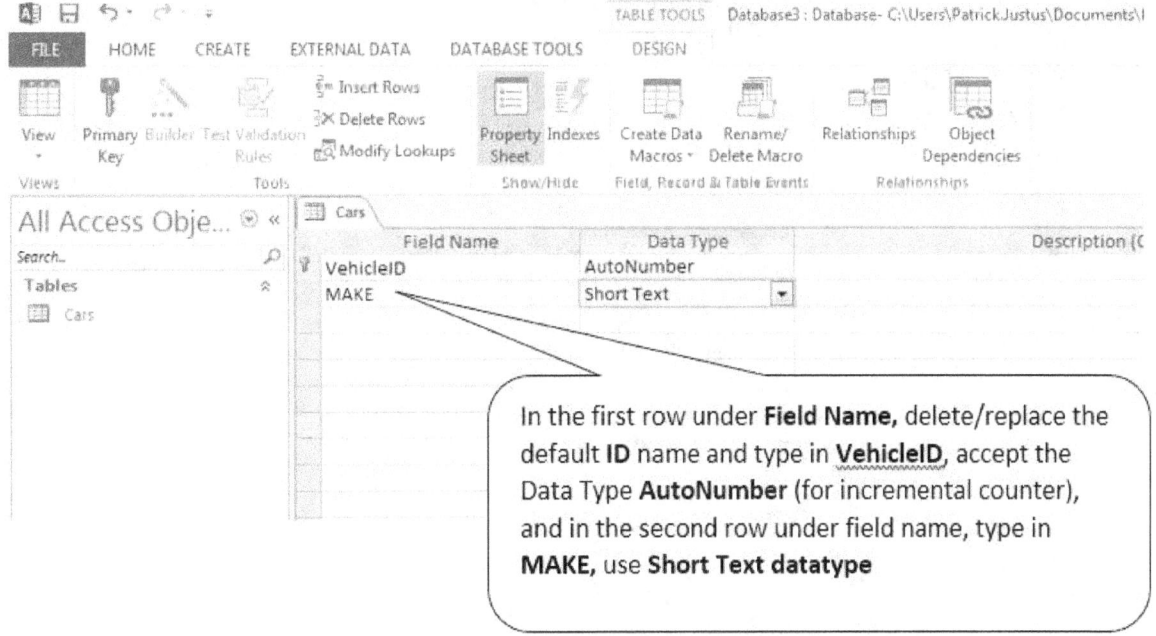

In the first row under **Field Name,** delete/replace the default **ID** name and type in **VehicleID**, accept the Data Type **AutoNumber** (for incremental counter), and in the second row under field name, type in **MAKE,** use **Short Text datatype**

Once you have keyed in the field name you then must say which **field width** or **field size** you wish that **FIELD** to have.

To do it correctly, you will need to know the longest **MAKE** of cars there is, and count the number of letters (this can be achieved through effective initial planning of the database design).

Click in the **field Properties** window under your structure and Access will highlight in black the figure **255.** This is the default filed width of all **Short Text** fields in this version of Access.

Press the delete key to remove the default figure 255, or type over it with the field width or size you need in relation to the database data fields..

Switch back to the Table window – top part of the screen.

Move across to the next column. The default in this column is **SHORT TEXT.** This is correct for **MAKE.**

The third column **Description box** is used for describing in more details the field you have just created. Optionally, you can leave this column blank.

Now continue with the rest of the database:

- Move down to the next line (just below MAKE)
- Key in **TYPE**
- Move to the next column. The default in this column is **Short Text.** This is correct for **Type**, so accept that.

Once you have keyed in the **Data Type** you then should say what field size you wish to **Field** to have.

- Move down into **Field Properties** window and change the field size to **20**

- Move back to the table window.
- Move down to next line (just below **Type**)
- Key in **PRICE**
- Move to the data type column; select **Currency** form the drop-down list.
- Move into **Field Properties** window and change decimal places to **2** as shown:

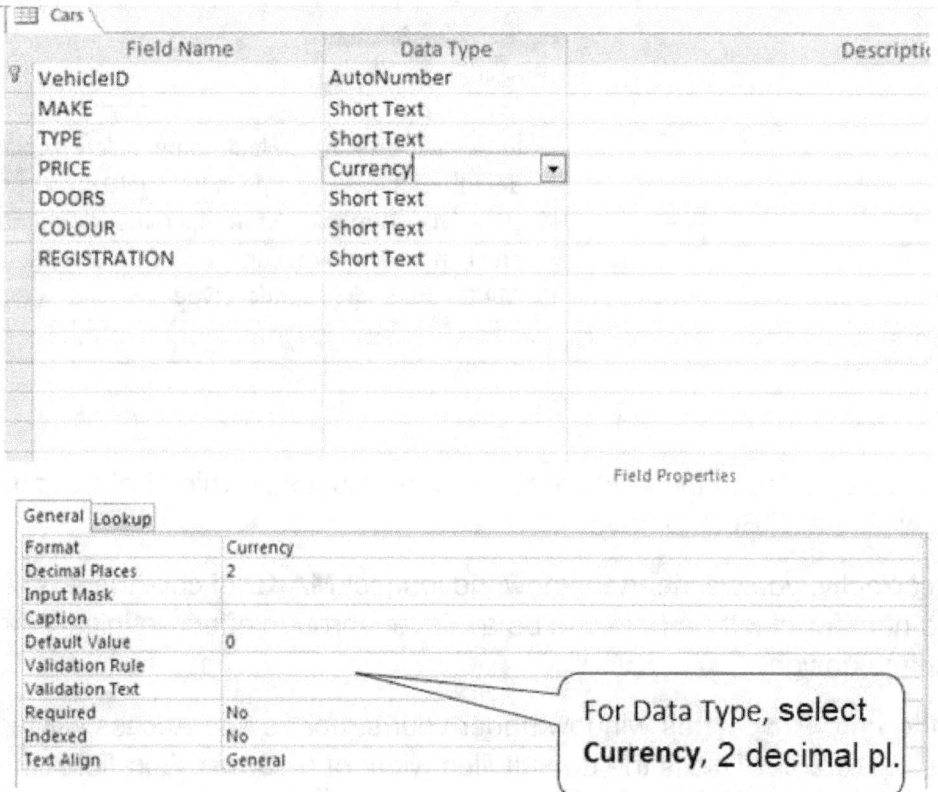

- Move back up to the Table Window (just above Field properties)
- Move down to the next line (just below Price)

- Key in **DOORS**
- Move to the data type column; select **Number** form the drop-down list.
- Move into field properties windows change field size set to **Double** (selecting from the field size drop-down list).

Next:

- Move back up to the Table Window (just above Field properties)
- Move down to the next line (just below Doors)

- Key in **COLOUR**
- Move to the data type column; accept the default data type as **Short Text.**
- Move down into field properties windows and change field size to **10.**

Next:

- Move back up to the Table Window
- Move down to the next line (just below Colour)

- Key in **REGISTRATION**
- Move to the data type column; again, accept the default data type as **Short Text** – (note that the data to be held under Registration are numbers, they are codes and a not values)
- Move down into field properties windows and change field size to **5.**
- Finally, move back up to the Table Window.

Once all fields have been set up you will need to SAVE the structure

1.4.3. Saving Your Database Structure

- Click on **File**
- Click on **SAVE AS**
- **SAVE AS** dialogue box appears on screen.
- If not already saved, change the default filename, **TABLE1** to read **CARSALES** by overtyping on it; (if prompted to save the table or database at any time, respond as required).
- Click on **OK** button and wait whilst saving takes place

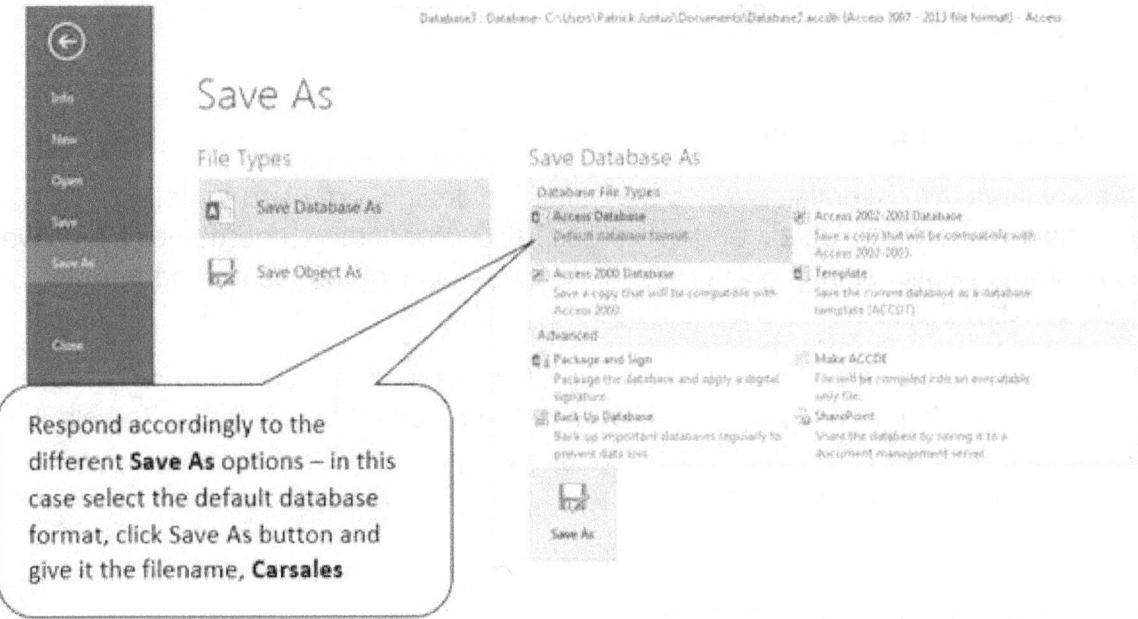

Implemented Design View of the Cars Database Structure

When the above is done correctly, a saved database structure, known as Design View of the Cars Database Structure would be displayed as shown below:

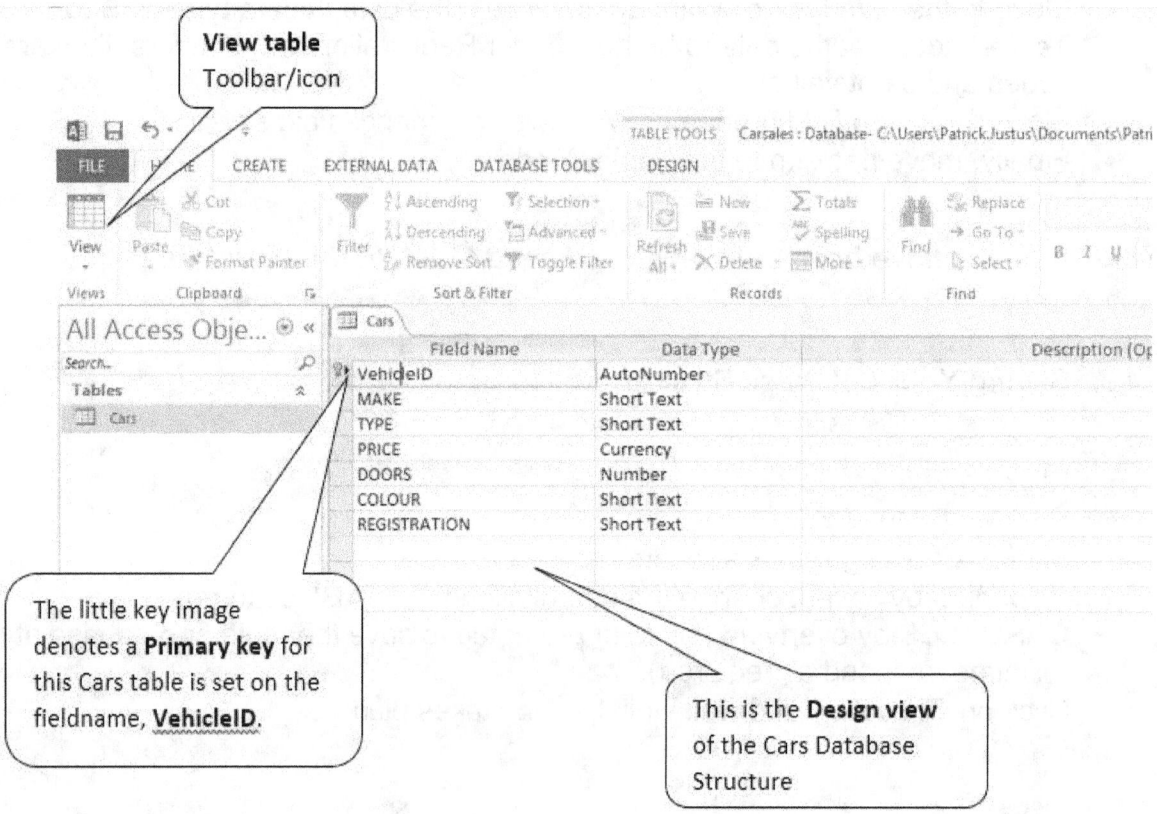

A note about Primary Keys

Primary keys are essential for effective database design, are used to define associations between tables, and serve as indexes for finding records quickly as well as to create relationships between tables in a relational database management system (RDBMS).

Any column that is selected as the primary key must have a record entry when the table is filled with entries; it must be NULL-free and cannot be omitted or left blank. Because they ensure that each record in the database is unique, primary keys are also known as unique identifiers.

1.4.4. Entering Data into a Table

Once you have saved your data structure, you can store information in the table. To do this, click on View Toolbar/Icon; and the **Table: CARS** window should appear as shown:

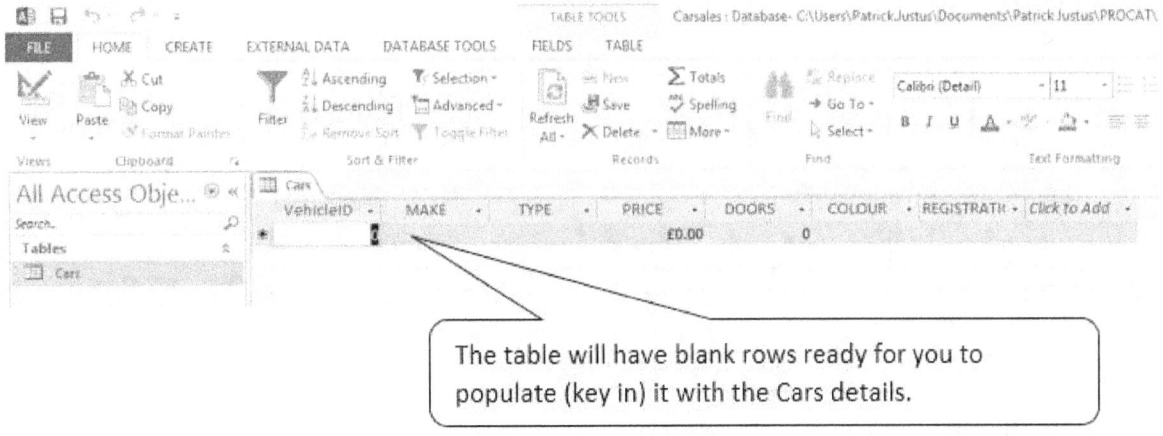

The table will have blank rows ready for you to populate (key in) it with the Cars details.

In the first row of the **Table: Cars,** denoted by the entry point image 'asterisk (*)', do the following accordingly:

- Key in **FORD** under the fieldname, **MAKE**
- Key in **ESCORT** under the fieldname, **TYPE**
- Key in **5000** under the fieldname, **PRICE**
- Key in **3** under the fieldname, **DOORS**
- Key in **RED** under the fieldname, **COLOUR**
- Key in **56** under the fieldname, **REGISTRATION**
- Press **ENTER**

Repeat the above process for all vehicles in the company Carsales list until all data has been inserted (see list of cars in the image below). Notice that as you enter your data for each record, the entry for **VehicleID** is automatically incremented - this is because the **Data type** was set as **AutoNumber** in the design of the database structure.

Once you have entered all 15 vehicle records for your table you will need to save it (if not already saved); No filename will be required because you have given it a filename earlier on. The completed Car Database should now look like this:

Diagram of the list of Cars in the database

To Print the Database:

- Take a screenshot or **Print out** the contents of car table in the usual Windows way.

2. Manipulating the Database

2.1. Adding New Records to a Database

When a new or used, car comes into the company for sale, the database would need to be updated by adding a new record. Follow the instructions below to add a new record:

- Open the Table: **CARS**
- Click on **Home | New** icon in the records ribbon (if not already displayed)
- At the record insertion point for VehicleID next to the field name MAKE column, Access displays a blank record with the term New highlighted in black.
- Key in **Vauxhall**
- Tab to the next field; key in **Astra 1.9**
- Tab to the next field; key in **8500**
- Tab to the next field; key in **3**
- Tab to the next field; key in **White**
- Tab to the next field; key in **15**
- Move to the next record of the first field (or record insertion point) in the table
- Notice that your record number (see below the table) is incremented by one record accordingly.

2.2.   Saving an Added Record

In Access, once you have entered a new record and moved to the **first field** of the next record. The previous record is automatically **saved**. **Print a copy** of your table showing the new record added. However, for assurance, you could click on the **Save** icon in the quick access area above the menus or press the F12 key.

2.3.   Deleting a Record

If for any reason you wish to delete the record of any car from the database, follow the instructions below:

To delete say, **record 6** from the Table: **Cars** database; click the cursor on to **record 6** and follow either of these 2 steps:

- Select or highlight record 6
- Under the record ribbon, click on the **Delete** picklist
- Click on **Select Delete Record**
- **Respond** accordingly - the caution dialogue box "**...you are about to delete one (1) record...**" will be displayed for you to confirm deletion or not (see image below).
- Choose **Yes** to save your changes or **No** to undo your changes.
- Click on the **Yes** button

OR

- Select or highlight record 6 and tap the **Delete Key**
- **Respond** accordingly - the caution dialogue box "**...you are about to delete one (1) record...**" will be displayed for you to confirm deletion or not (see image below).
- Choose **Yes** to save your changes or **No** to undo your changes.
- Click on the **Yes** button

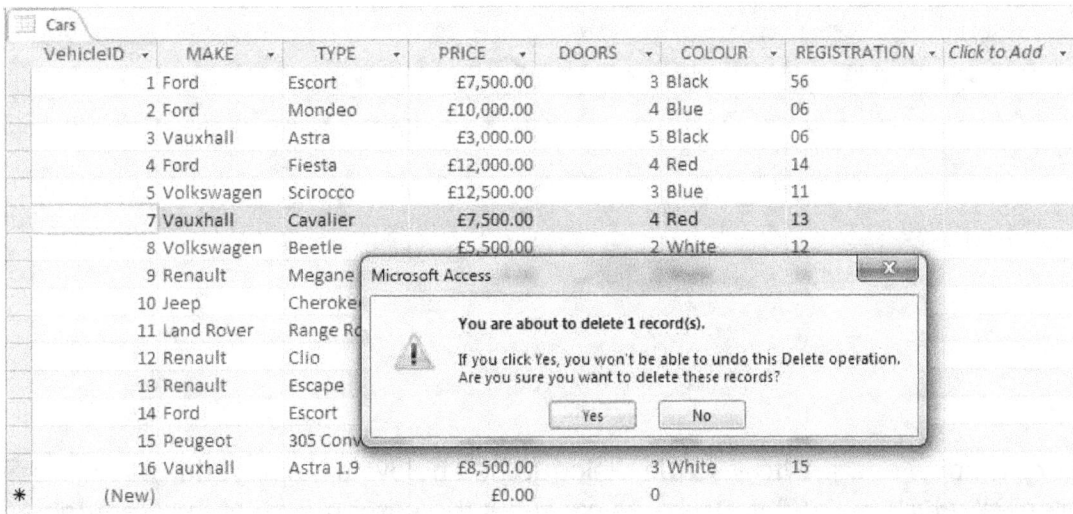

- Notice that record 6 has vanished along with its primary key.

Try this again; delete **record 7** from your database in the same way; and save your database when done.

Note that deleting records from a database must only be carried out when you are certain and sure of what you are about to do – records deleted cannot be recovered.

2.4. Saving a database table
- Click on **FILE**
- Click on **SAVE TABLE**
- No filename is required as you have earlier named it.
- However, for assurances, you could click on the **Save** icon in the quick access area above the menus or press the F12 key.

Database Manipulation Activity

2.5. Sorting

Your database can be sorted using Access either numerically or alphabetically. You can accomplish this in a number of ways, including using the Home menu, the Sort & Filter ribbon, or a query where you can specify the field(s) you wish to sort your database on.

To try this using the **query** option; open or load your **Table: Cars** in table view format.

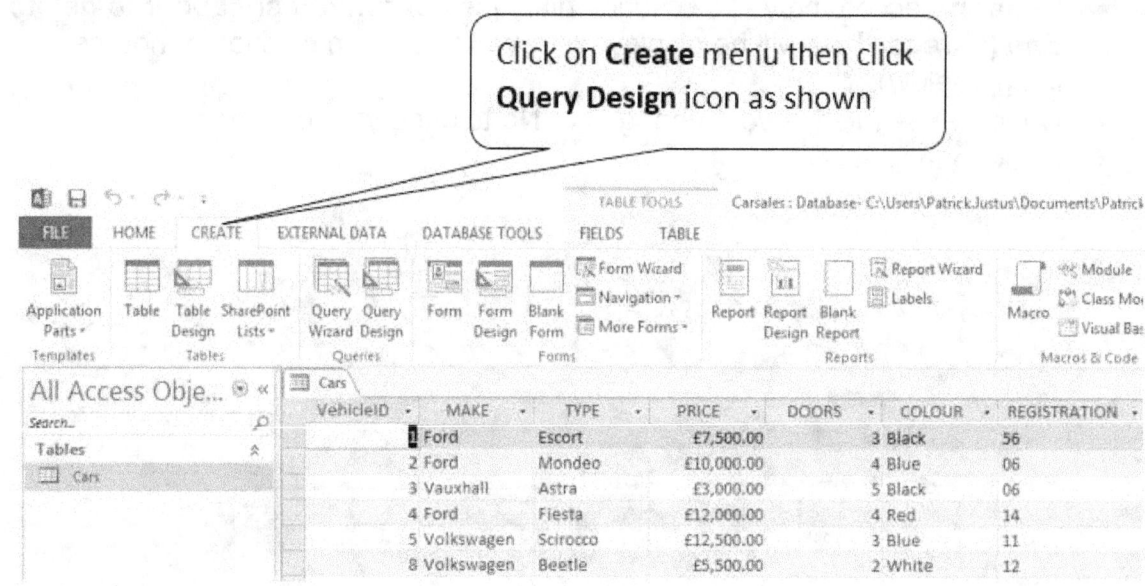

The **Query** window and a **Show Table** dialogue box below is displayed from where you can select which table(s) you wish to carry out the sort on. Select the Cars table from this dialogue box and click **Add** to add the Cars Table structure onto the space in the centre of the window as shown below and then click on the **Close** button to close the small dialogue box.

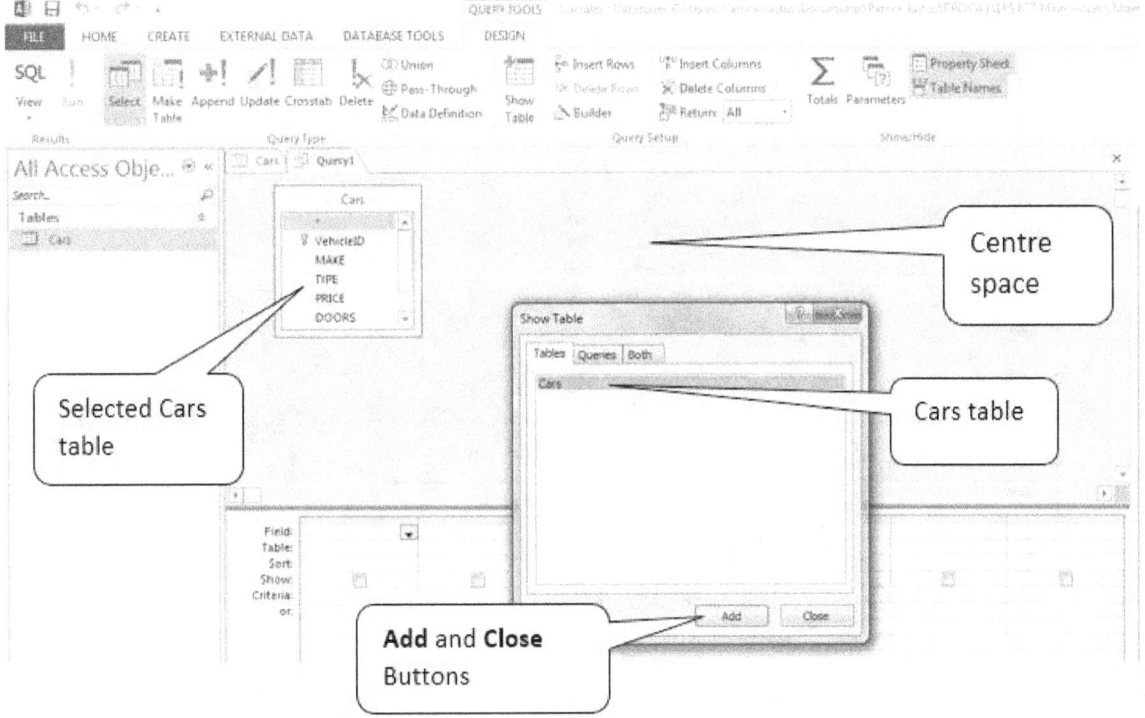

Now, carry out either of the following processes:

- drag and drop each field successively onto the column rows marked **Field:**
OR

- Double click on each fieldname successively and the same fieldname will appear in the **Field:** (first row and column);
OR

- you can also click on each picklist in the **Field:** (first row and column), and select the desired fieldname(s) respectively.

- Then to carry out the **Sort**; click on the third row, under the field you wish to carry out the sort on; select Ascending or Descending order from the picklist shown
- Select the table columns you want to appear in the sort results by checking or unchecking the **Show** checkboxes.
- See and follow infographics steps in the query definition window below:

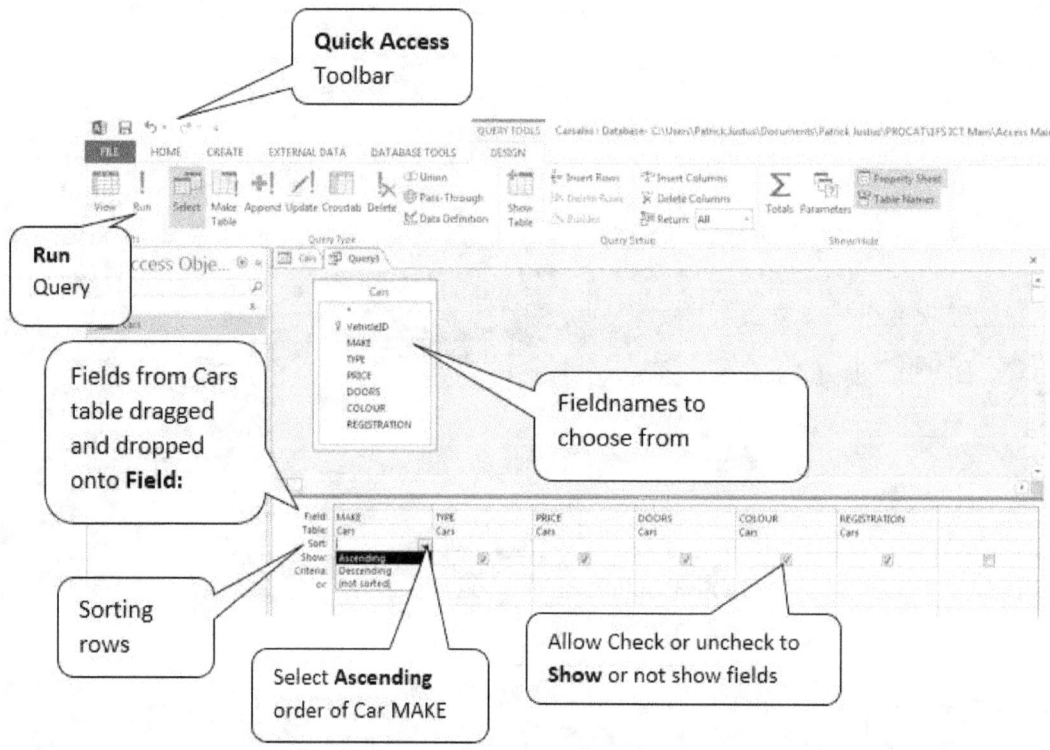

Note: This diagram is known as the query definition window

- To sort Cars database by **MAKE**, click on the blank cell in the same column/row next to the word **Sort:**
- A small picklist (downward arrow) appears on the blank cell
- Click on the picklist and select the word **ASCENDING.** This will put your database result into Alphabetical order of the **MAKE** column.

In the various field columns along the row titled, **Show:** notice that the checkboxes for all selected fields are checked by default. This ensures that the data in that field is shown on the table view. Should you not want to show data for any field, then uncheck the checkbox for that field.

- Ignore the rows for **CRITERIA** and **OR** at this stage.
- To view the **sorted** Cars table; click on the **Run Query** icon.

When the above is done correctly, your table should appear on the screen displayed in an **alphabetical order** of MAKE.

You may now **Save** the query:

- Click on the **Save icon** in the **Quick Access Toolbars** OR Press F12 key OR
- Click on **File | SAVE QUERY AS**
- Delete or overtype the default **query1** name and name it **Sorted by Make.**
- Click the **OK** button
- Print out or take a screenshot of your sorted table

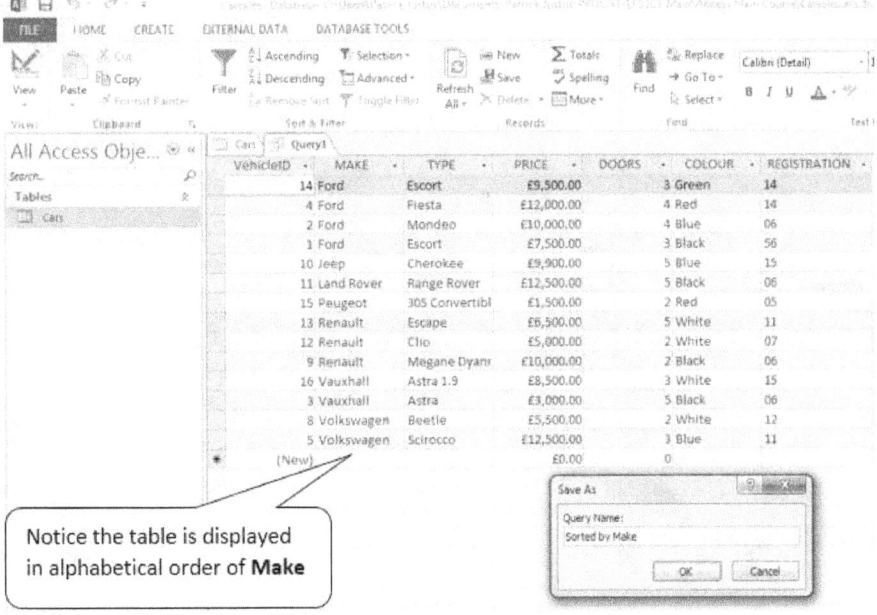

Notice the table is displayed in alphabetical order of **Make**

2.6. Search (Query) the Database on a Specific Criteria

Access allows you to search your table for records which meet certain conditions or criteria;

- *Let us search the database for '**List of All Cars valued under £7,500.00**':*

2.6.1. Solutions - *'List of All Cars valued under £7,500.00'*

- To do this we will need to set up a new query based on Table: **Cars**
- Repeat the entire process for sorting a database as explained above making sure all field names are selected for the query.
- At the **query definition window**, carry out the following:
  - At the '**Criteria:**' intersection cell with the **PRICE** field (see image below)
  - Key in **<7500**
  - Click on **Run Query** icon to display your Query result
  - **Print** out or take a **screenshot** of the Query result
  - **Save** the query using the filename '**Cars less than £7,500**'

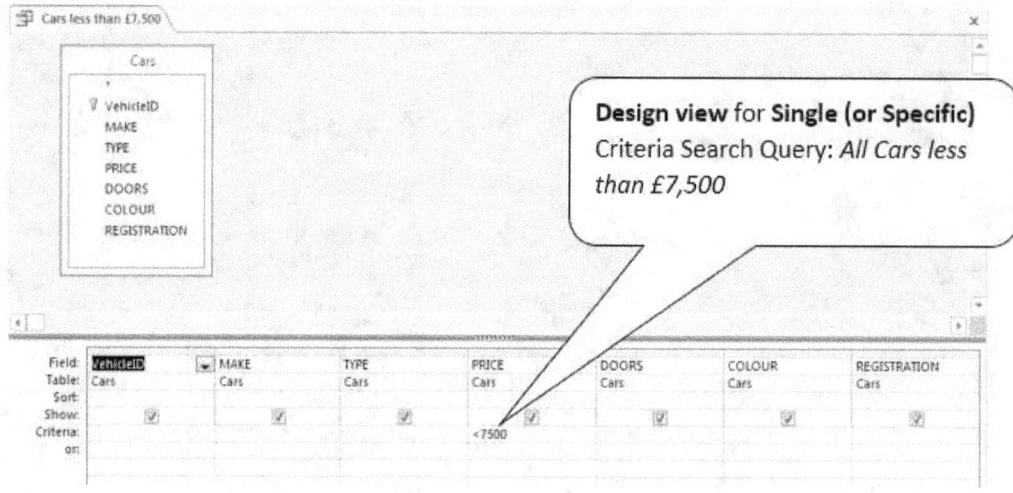

Design view for **Single (or Specific)** Criteria Search Query: *All Cars less than £7,500*

Query Result:

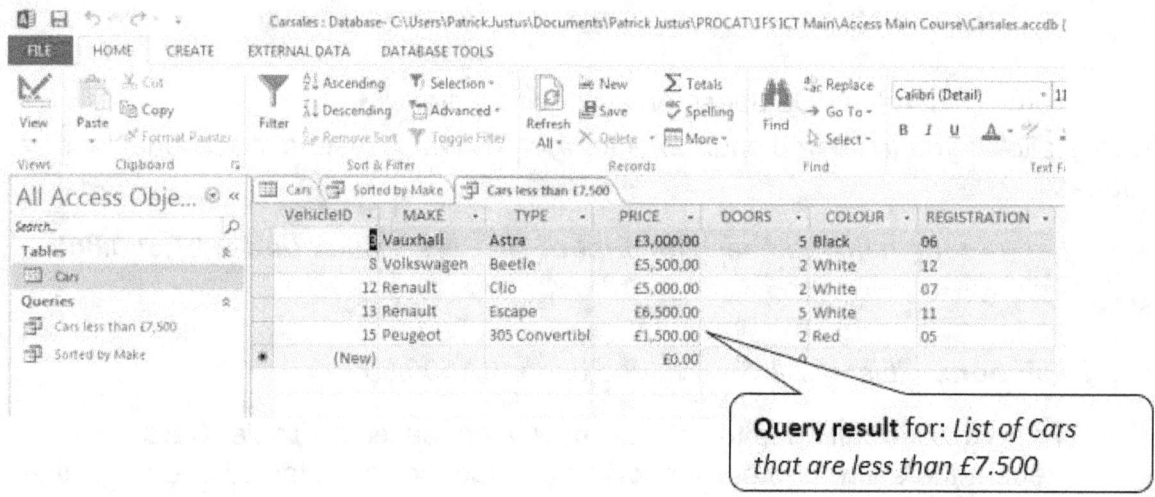

Query result for: *List of Cars that are less than £7.500*

2.7. Search (Query) the Database on a Multiple Criteria

- *Let us search the database for '**All Ford Cars that are less than a given amount**'*

2.7.1. Solutions - *All Ford Cars that are less than a given amount*

- Set up a new query based on Table: **Cars**

- Repeat the **query process** as detailed above making sure all field names are selected for the query.
- At the **query definition window**, carry out the following:
  - At the **Criteria:** intersection cell with the **MAKE** field (see image below)
  - Key in **Ford**
  - Still on the **Criteria:** row, move to the intersection cell with the **PRICE** field
  - Type this in including the square bracket; "**< [Enter Price:]**"

- o Then click on **Run Query** icon
- o **Print** out or take a **screenshot** of the Query result
- o **Save** the query using the filename **'Ford Cars less than a given Price'**

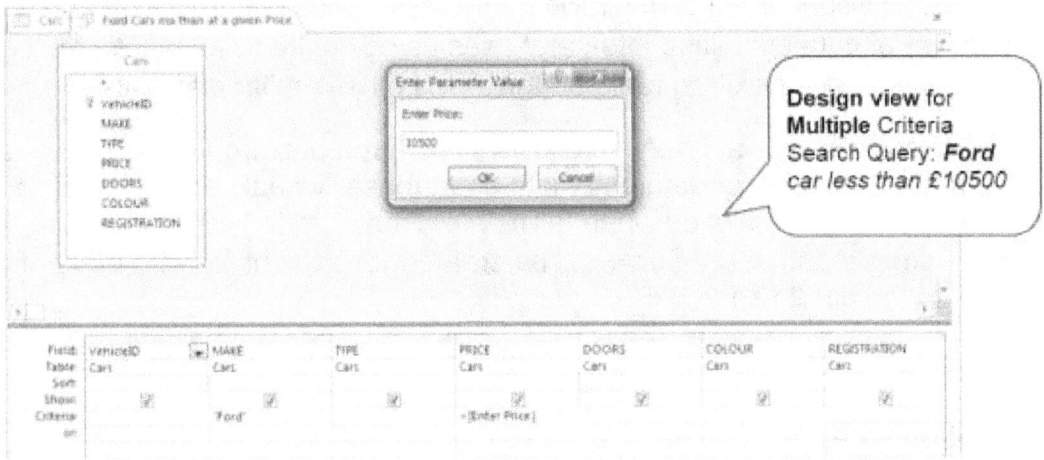

Query Result:

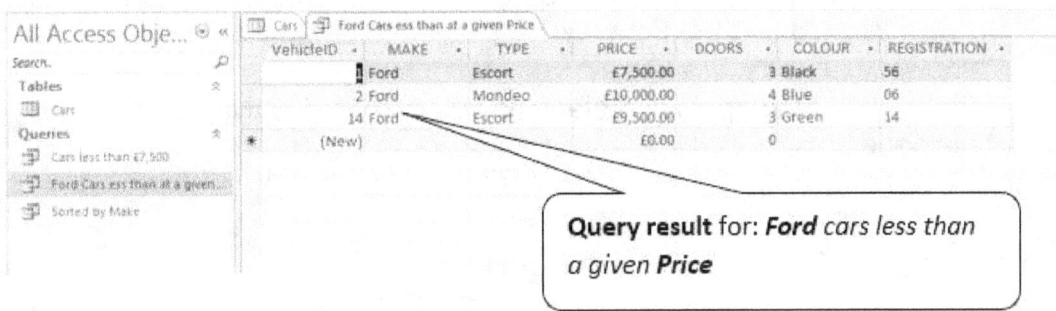

Query result for: *Ford* cars less than a given *Price*

2.8.   Consolidation

Now, try these; search for other Cars from the database that matches the following criteria and print out or take screenshots of your results:

1. List all Cars that are White in colour and less than £9000
2. List all Cars with 2 doors
3. List all Cars with a given number of doors
4. List all Cars registered after a given year *(e.g. 06 for 2006)*
5. List any Car details using the vehicle's ID
6. List a Car by its Make using only the first two characters (i.e. use of wildcard) e.g. **Ho*** for Honda
7. List a Car's year of registration showing only the Vehicle's ID, Make, Model and year of Registration, e.g. recall the use of '**Show**'.

3. Form Creation

3.1. Why Create a Form?

The entry of data is done using forms in Access. In order to enter and display data in a database, Forms offers a graphical user interface (GUI), sometimes known as visual prompts. It allows for the assurance of the validity and integrity of data submitted into databases using controls like labels, textboxes, drop-down lists, picklists, radio buttons, and other similar elements.

- Using **Forms** in a database allows visual prompts, drop down boxes, and makes it easier for data entry into a database. Visual verification of data entry can be achieved when forms are used.
- A **simple** data entry **Form** will be created for straight forward entry of data into the database.

3.2. To Create a Form

Follow these steps to create a simple **Form** on a Table:

Step 1:

- Ensure the **Table: Cars** is opened;
- Click on **Create** on the menu bar to reveal the **Form** ribbon; then click on **Form Wizard** and the Form Wizard dialogue box will be displayed as shown
- Follow the infographic and steps as you carry out activities within the dialogue box:

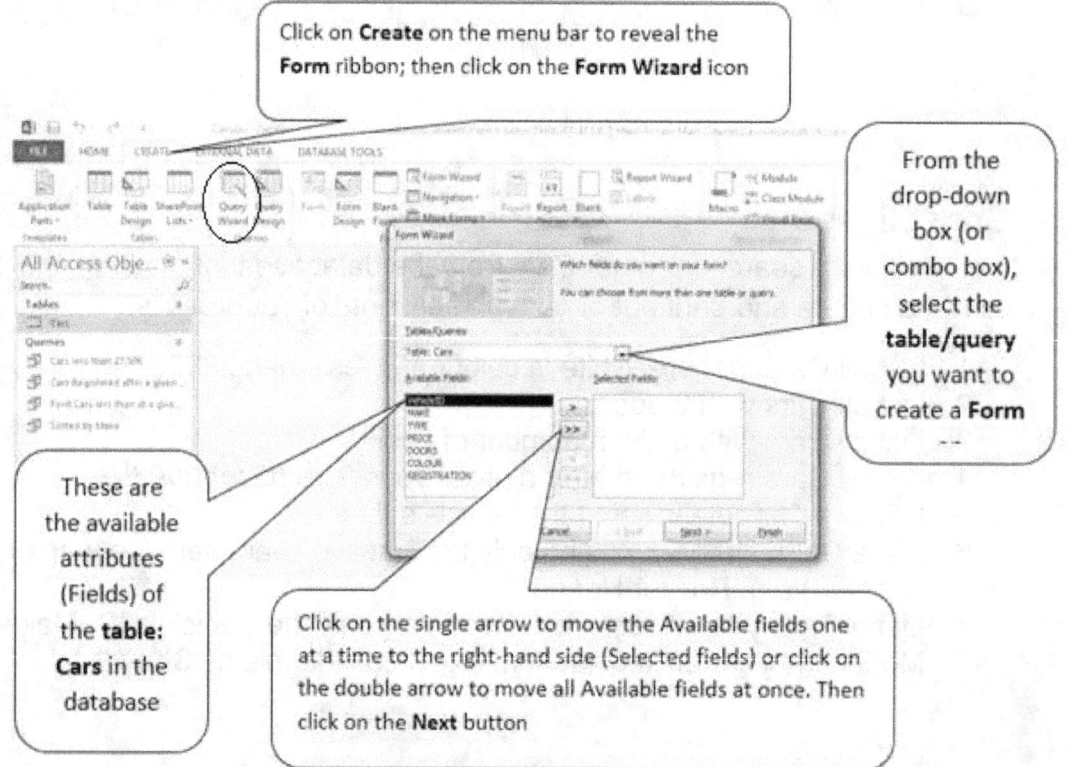

Click on **Create** on the menu bar to reveal the **Form** ribbon; then click on the **Form Wizard** icon

From the drop-down box (or combo box), select the **table/query** you want to create a **Form**

These are the available attributes (Fields) of the **table: Cars** in the database

Click on the single arrow to move the Available fields one at a time to the right-hand side (Selected fields) or click on the double arrow to move all Available fields at once. Then click on the **Next** button

Step 2:

- With the **Next** button clicked in step 1
- the next stage of the **Form Wizard** dialogue box is displayed:

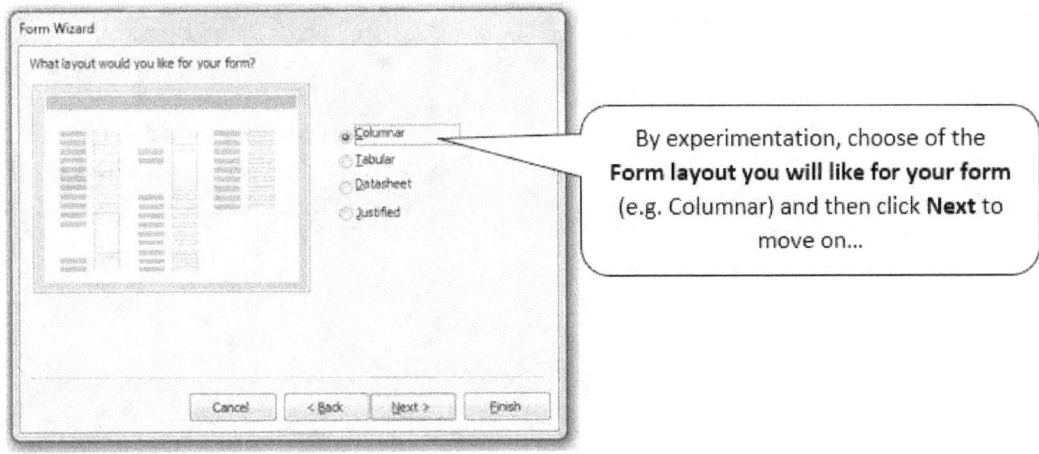

By experimentation, choose of the **Form layout you will like for your form** (e.g. Columnar) and then click **Next** to move on...

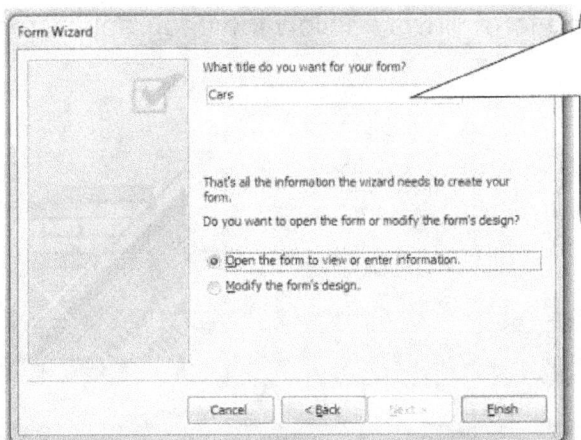

Specify **what title you want for your form;** either accept the default title, Cars or overtype it with a new title (e.g. Car Details). Then Click on the **Finish** button to **open the form to view or enter information** as required.

Step 3:

- With the **Finish** button clicked in step 2;
- the finished **Form GUI** is displayed (which may need to be tweaked/tidied up);
- when completed, click on **Save** icon to save the created form (the **form** name already assigned or provided before the finished button was clicked above).

The finished form (before any adjustments) is displayed below:

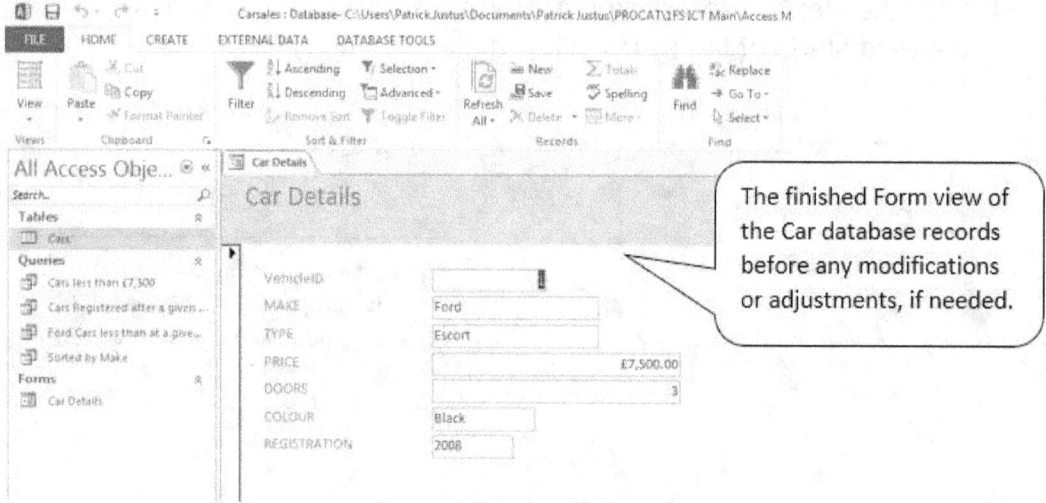

The finished Form view of the Car database records before any modifications or adjustments, if needed.

Attention: In the **Form GUI**, notice that the **Textboxes** are somewhat far apart from the **Labels** and that the textboxes also have long and irregular widths. This can be corrected and tidied up by switching to the **Form Design view.** The diagrams below show the form design view and finished form views – follow the infographic steps and instructions:

3.2.1. The Form Design View:

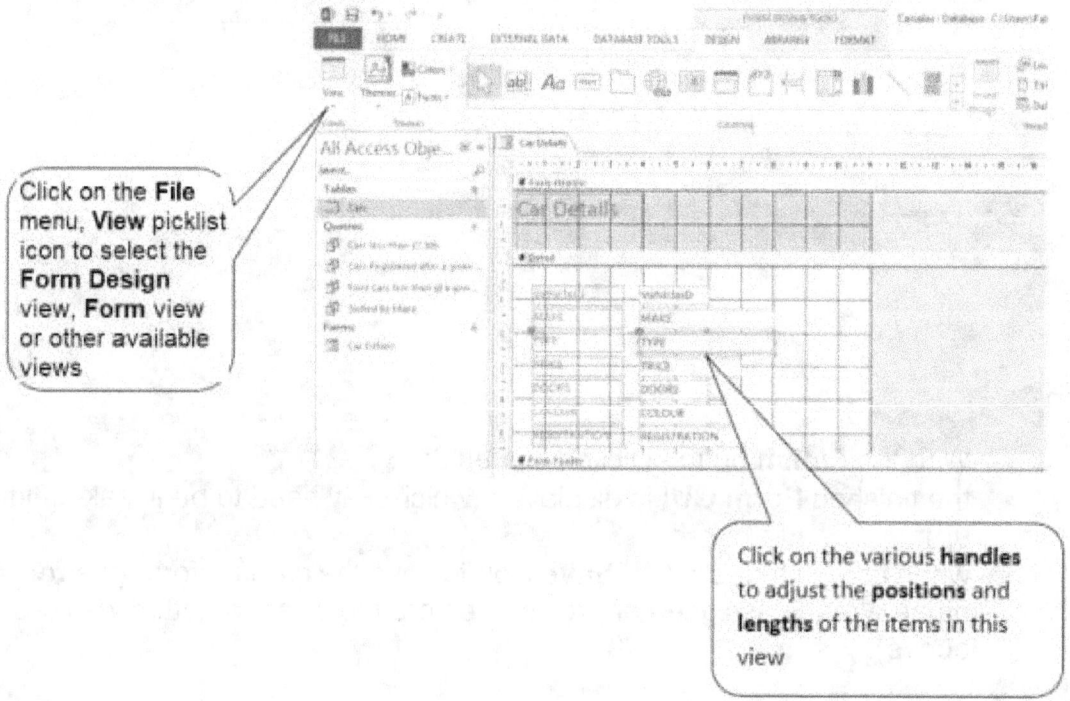

Click on the **File** menu, **View** picklist icon to select the **Form Design** view, **Form** view or other available views

Click on the various **handles** to adjust the **positions** and **lengths** of the items in this view

3.2.2. The finished Form View:

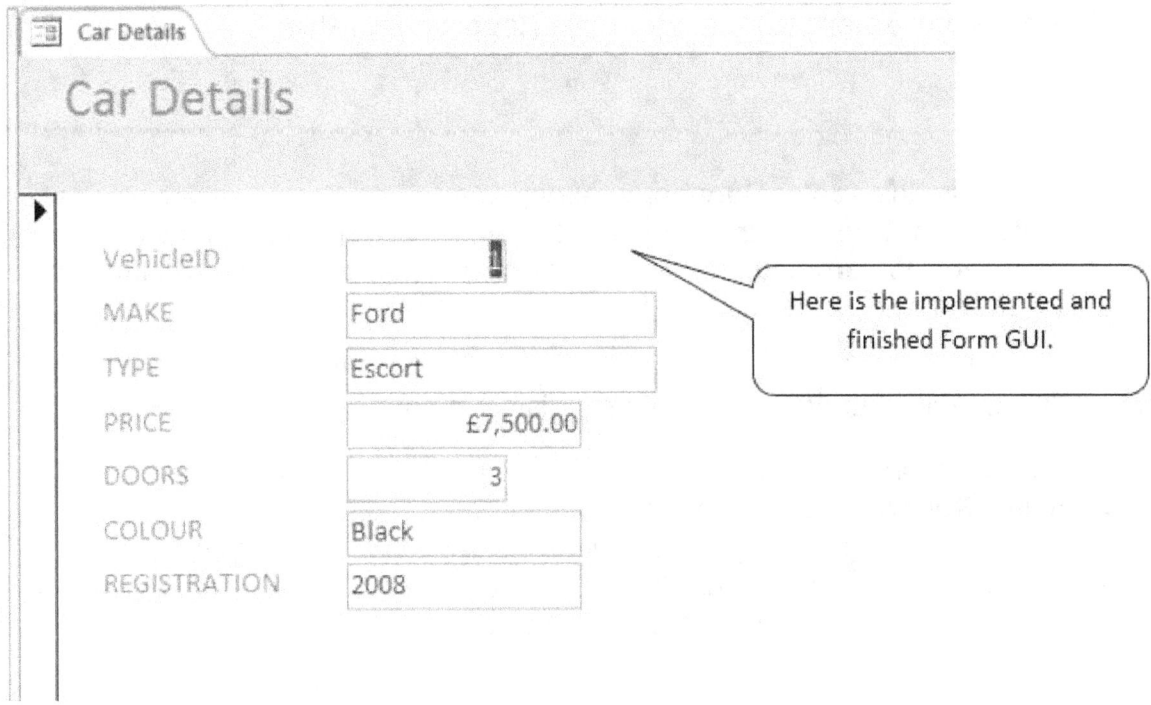

Here is the implemented and finished Form GUI.

Stretch and Challenge Activity

Exploratory activity - carry out the following activities where necessary:

- For data entry validation, consider using message box comments, data entry validation, etc.
- Password protection can be used to log into a database system.
- There may also be a password for carrying out data updates.
- For security, many levels of passwords may be required to access a database.
- More complex functions can be introduced and attained by writing custom control types and codes.
- There will be an application verification feature in the form of a warning dialogue box for determining whether the user wishes to commit to a specific action, such as quitting an application.
- As a final feature, a Switchboard will be able to be launched as the initial Form when the database system is run, utilising the reserved name command "Autoexec" in this case.
- Future developments may include the addition of other features that were not included in this project, such as the ability to hide all database tools as well as navigation, creation, and editing controls.

4. Report Creation

4.1.   Follow these steps to create a simple **Report** on a Table:

Step 1:

- Ensure the **Table: Cars** are opened;
- Click on **Create** on the menu bar to reveal the **Report** ribbon; then click on **Report Wizard** and the Report Wizard dialogue box will be displayed as shown below:

Take steps carrying out activities within the dialogue box:

- Select the **Create** menu tab
- Select **Report Wizard** from the Reports ribbon
- the Report Wizard dialogue box will be displayed as shown below
- Take steps carrying out activities within the dialogue box – *making sure to follow the infographic instructions at each step:*

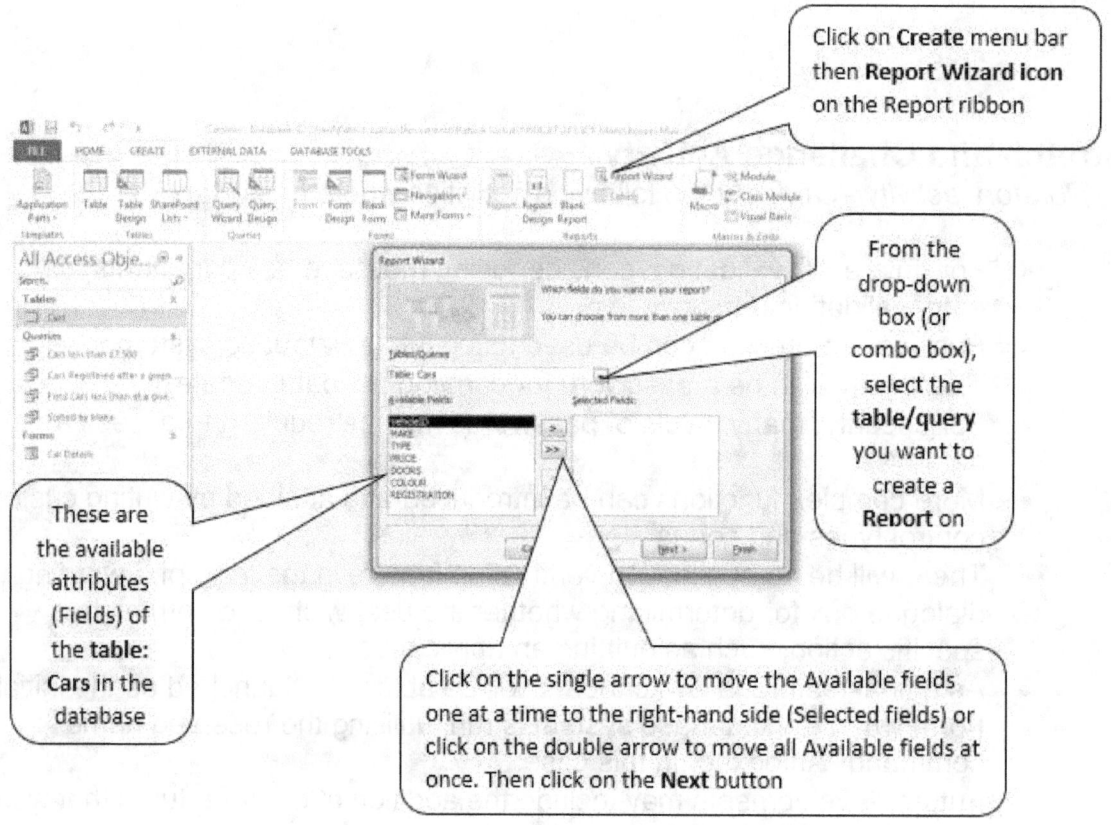

Click on **Create** menu bar then **Report Wizard icon** on the Report ribbon

From the drop-down box (or combo box), select the **table/query** you want to create a Report on

These are the available attributes (Fields) of the **table: Cars** in the database

Click on the single arrow to move the Available fields one at a time to the right-hand side (Selected fields) or click on the double arrow to move all Available fields at once. Then click on the **Next** button

Report Wizard Dialogue box showing selected fields for the report:

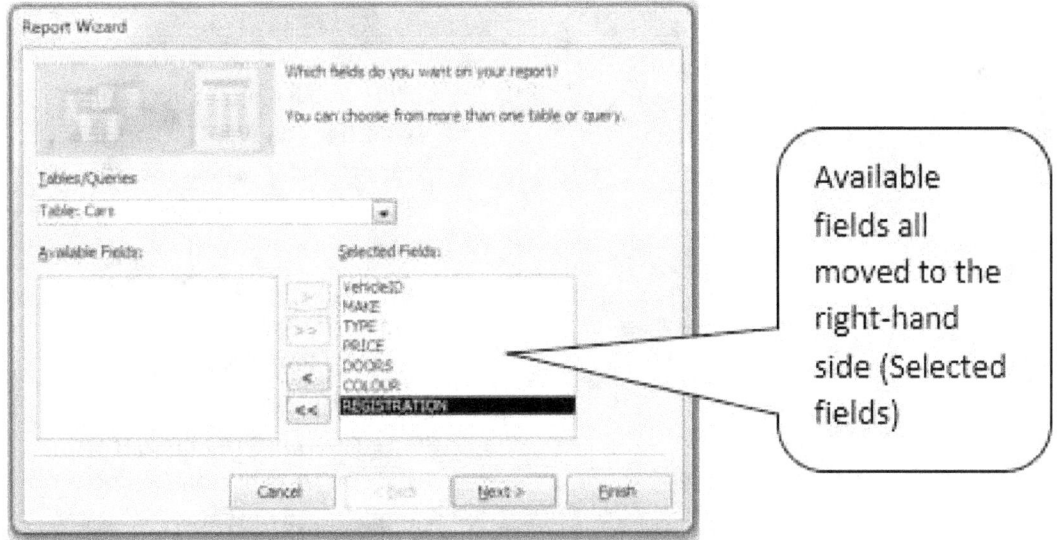

Step 2:

- With the **Next** button clicked in step 1;
- the next stage of the **Report Wizard** dialogue box is displayed;
- then click **Next** button

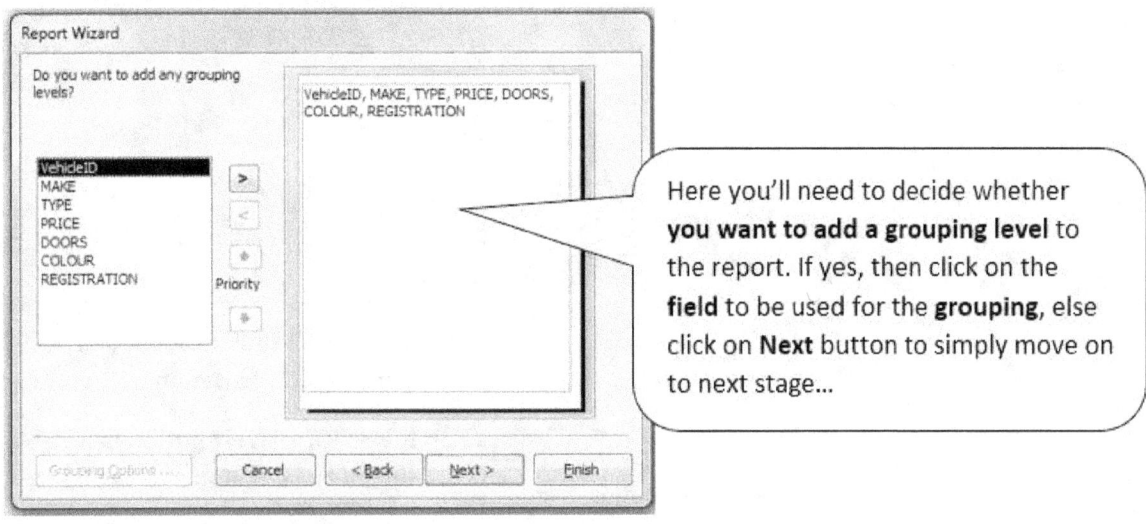

Step 3:

- With the **Next** button clicked in step 2;
- the **Sort Order** report wizard is displayed;
- then click **Next** button

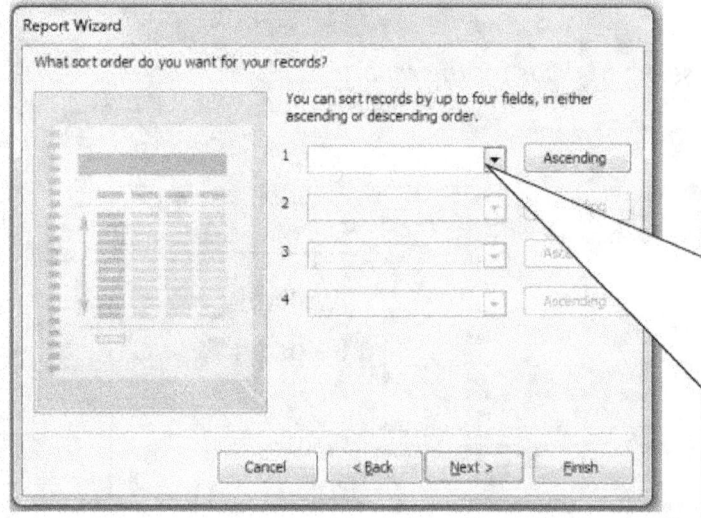

Here you'll need to decide whether **you want to sort the report and in which record order**. If yes, then click on the drop-down box and select the **field** to be used for the **sort** (you can sort record by up to four fields). Select **Ascending** or **Descending** order of sort; else if sort not required, then click on **Next** button to simply move on to next stage...

Step 4:

- With the **Next** button clicked in step 3;
- the **Report Layout** report wizard is displayed;
- Select the **Tabular Layout** and **Landscape Orientation**;
- then click **Next** button

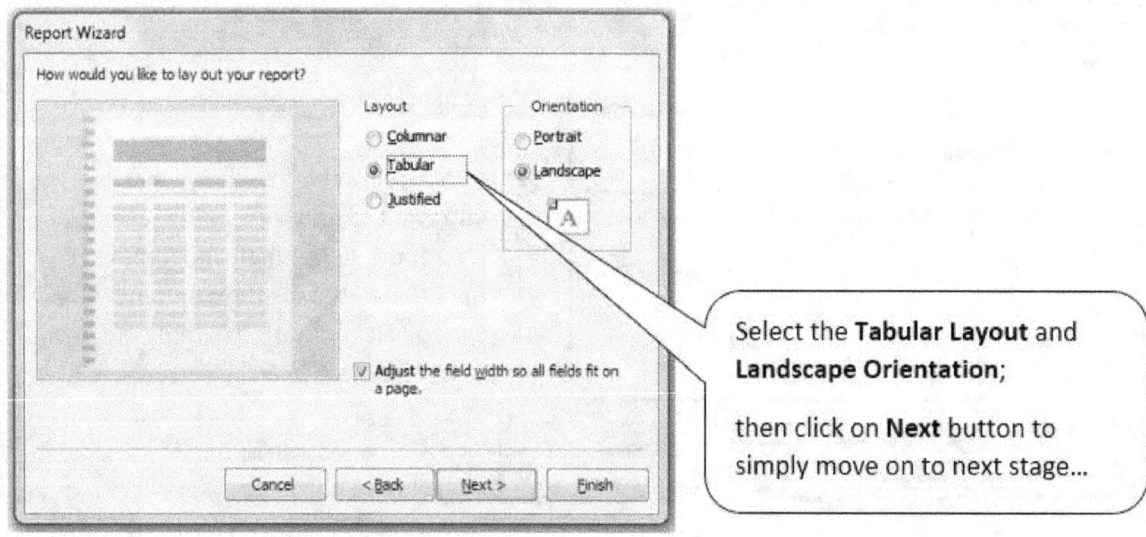

Select the **Tabular Layout** and **Landscape Orientation**;

then click on **Next** button to simply move on to next stage...

Step 5:

- With the **Next** button clicked in step 4;
- the **Report Title** report wizard is displayed;
- Specify the car title for the report;
- then click **Finish** button

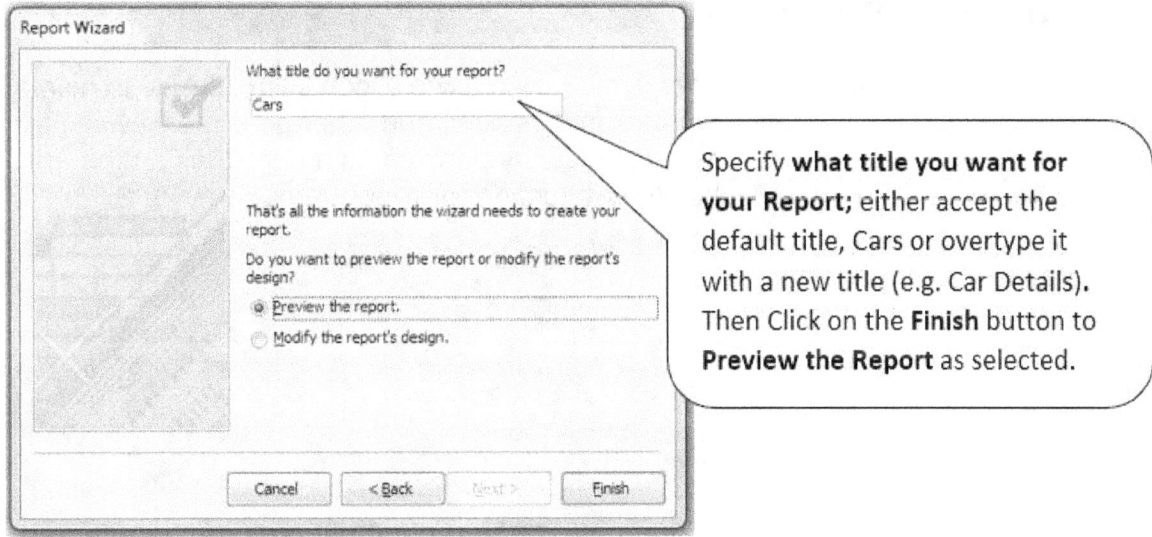

Specify **what title you want for your Report;** either accept the default title, Cars or overtype it with a new title (e.g. Car Details). Then Click on the **Finish** button to **Preview the Report** as selected.

Step 6:

- With the **Finish** button clicked in step 5;
- the finished **Report** is displayed (which may need to be tweaked/tidied up);
- when completed, click on **Save** icon to save the created Report (the **Report** name already assigned or provided before the finished button was clicked above).

The **Report** presented is spaced out too far apart with very wide column widths and part of the fields may be truncated

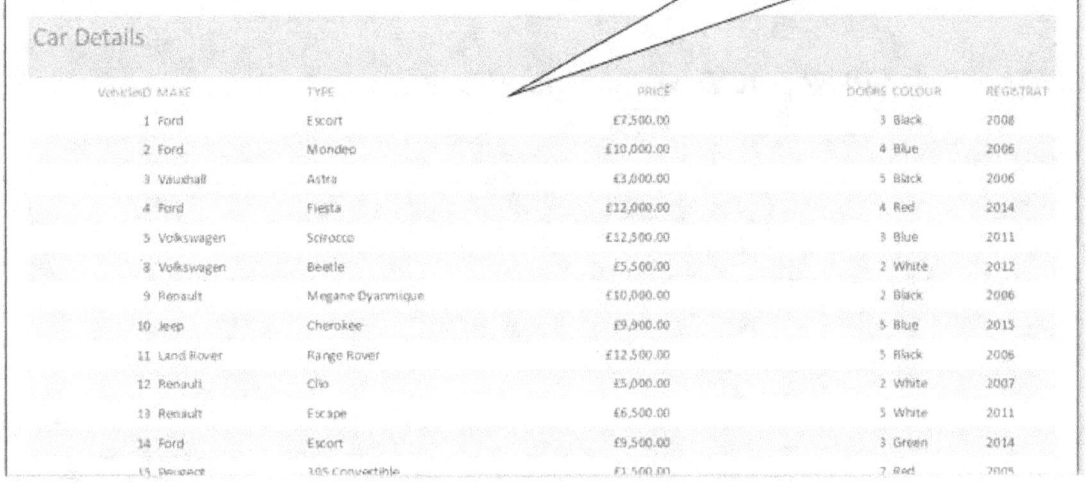

Attention: that the **Report** presented is spaced out too far apart with very wide column widths, and part of the field is truncated. The truncated fields must be corrected and tidied up by switching to the **Report Design view.** The diagrams below show the Report design view and finished Report views:

4.1.1. The Report Design View:

After choosing the Report menu, click on the View icon's tiny picklist to display the Report Design view, Report Print Preview, and other possible views. You can also access the report design view by performing a right-click on the completed Car Report in the Report section (or report tab).

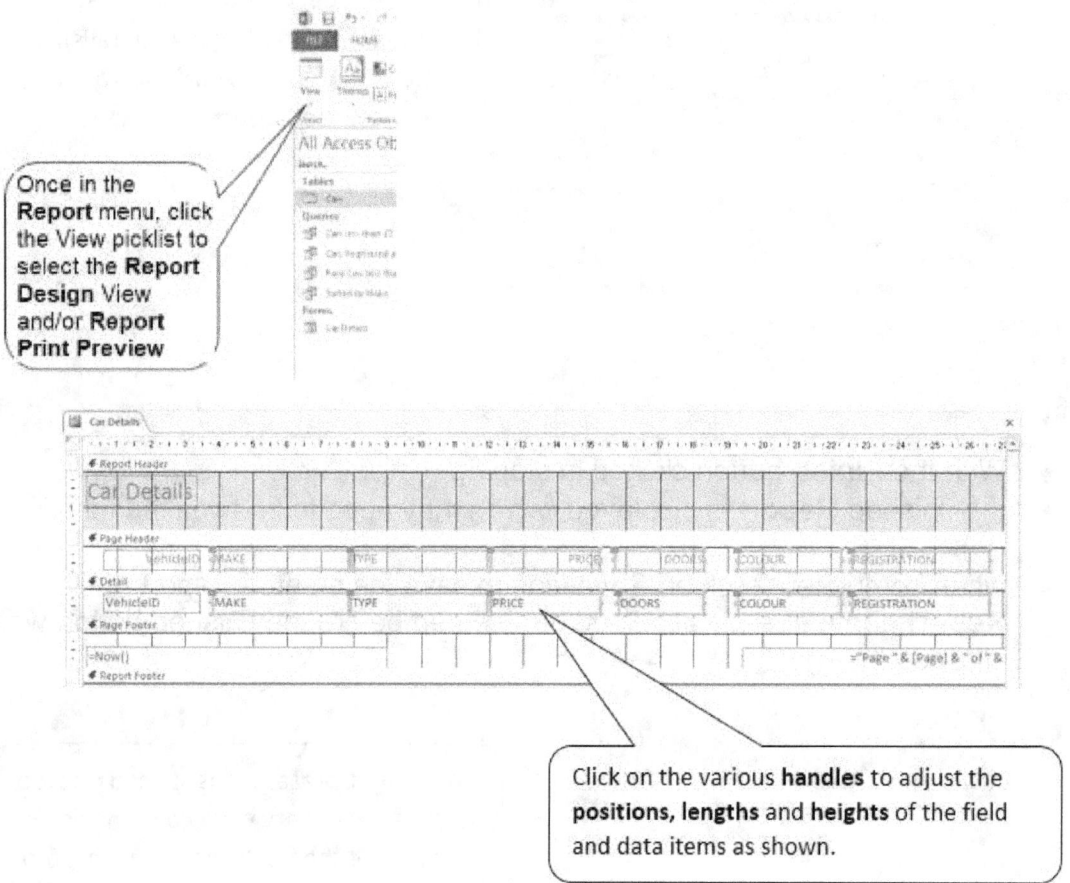

Once in the **Report** menu, click the View picklist to select the **Report Design** View and/or **Report Print Preview**

Click on the various **handles** to adjust the **positions, lengths** and **heights** of the field and data items as shown.

4.1.2. The Finished Report View (i.e. Print Preview):

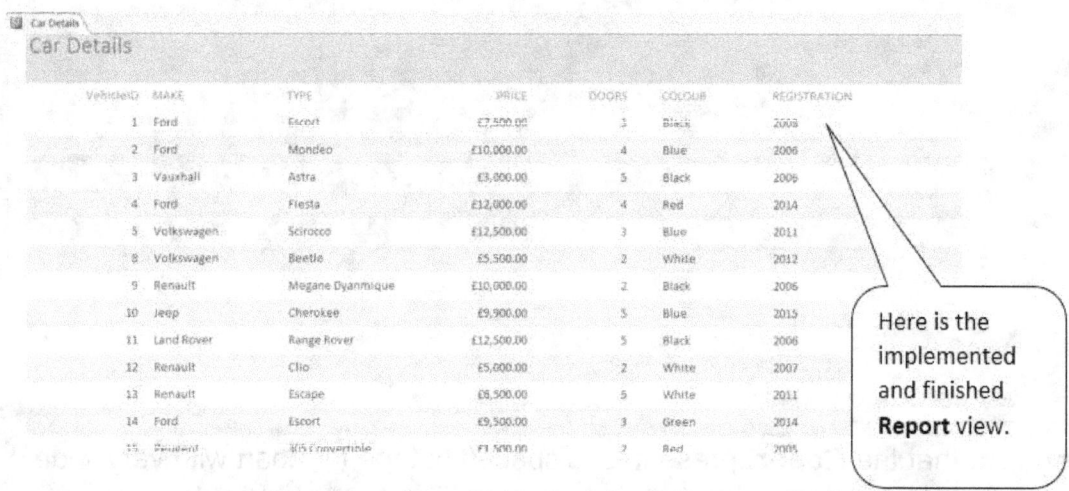

Here is the implemented and finished **Report** view.

4.1.3. Printing a report

If you are already within Print Preview, click the **Print** button on the Print Tool bar.

5. Closing the Database

- Click on **FILE** menu bar
- Click on **Close**

If you have made changes to your database structure e.g. added records/fields; deleted records/fields or edited information in any way and have not re-saved it, you will be prompted if you wish to save changes in the **CLOSE DIALOGUE BOX** – respond accordingly.

- Click on **YES or NO**
- Click on **CLOSE DATABASE**

5.1. To Exit the Access database:

- Click on **EXIT** button on the top right-hand corner of the application.

Importing data

Data import is helpful for studying, improving, and creating data models, among other things. Data can be imported using cut-and-paste, from a spreadsheet, or from a database.

From another excel worksheet, a word document, or other sources, data can be copied and pasted into an excel worksheet.

Locate and select the worksheet contents you want to import. Then, open the new worksheet to receive the imported data. Choose, for example, cell A1 and click paste (or enter Ctrl+V to paste the copied (or moved) data). The imported data can then be modified as needed.

Importing data from Access Database to Excel Spreadsheet

- The following steps can be taken to import data from an Access database into an Excel spreadsheet:
  - If a spreadsheet worksheet is not already open, open a new one and rename it, for example, "Students information";
  - Find the Import Access Data option under the Data|Get Data From Access menu bar ribbon.
  - Select the StudentDB file from the list of stored database files in Access, and then click the Import button.

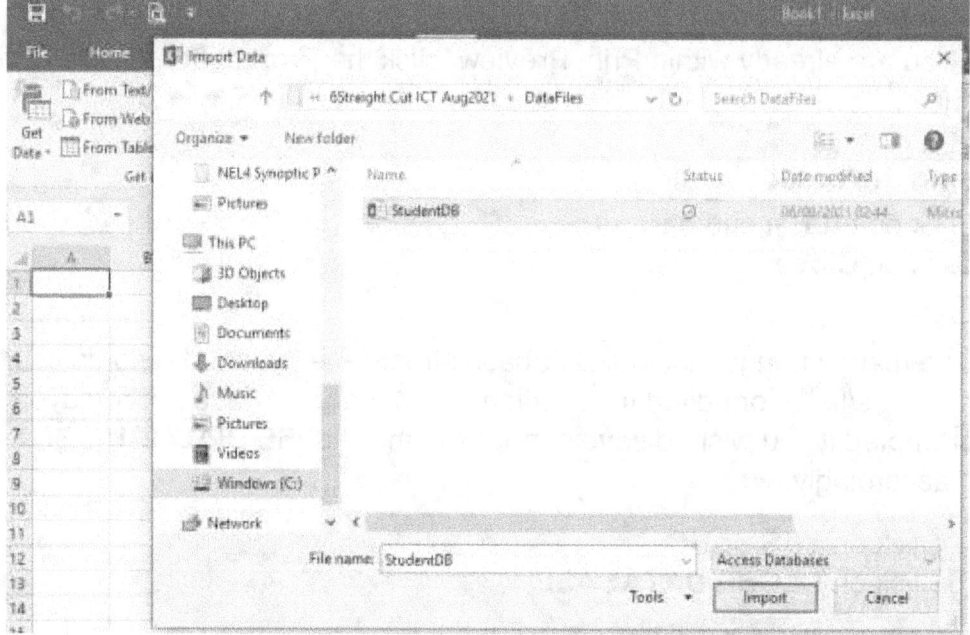

- After clicking on the import button, verify that the files are the right ones by checking or selecting the table of records in the Access box, then click the OK button.

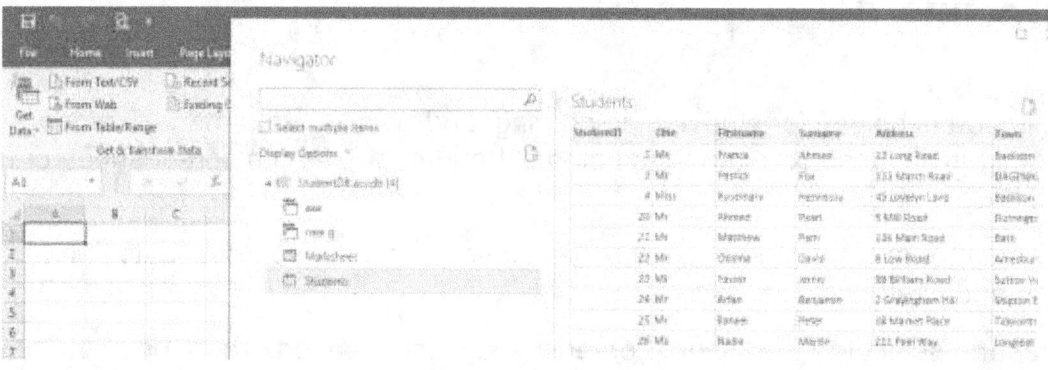

- Click Open after choosing/confirming the data import in cell A1 (which is already selected and is clearly visible).
- If the procedures below were properly completed, the Access Database file should now appear as follows in your Excel spreadsheet:

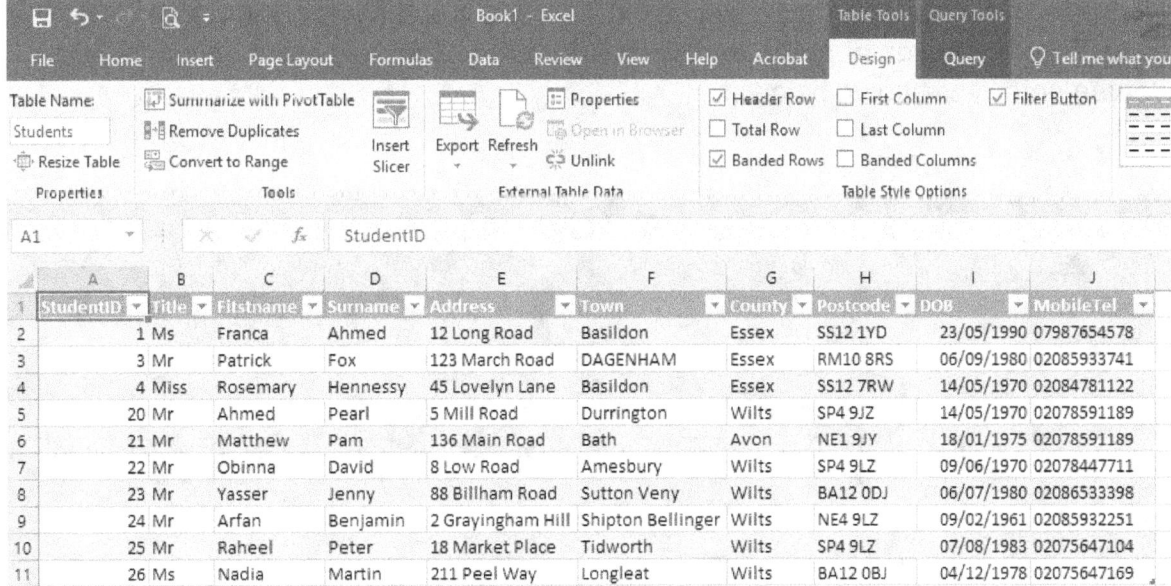

The above image is the Access database file or records that has been imported from Access into Excel spreadsheet.

Consolidation – Course Database

Instructions:

Launch/load a blank Access database in the usual way.

Save the database into a designated folder; give it a meaningful name e.g. *coursesDB*, then click on the **CREATE** button to create the database.

You will be presented with the database **design view** where you should create the following **database structure**:

- Course Code (text, 8)
- Course Title (text, 30)
- Course Fee (currency, standard, 2pl)
- Room Number (number, integer)

Below is the implemented database structure showing the fieldnames and data types:

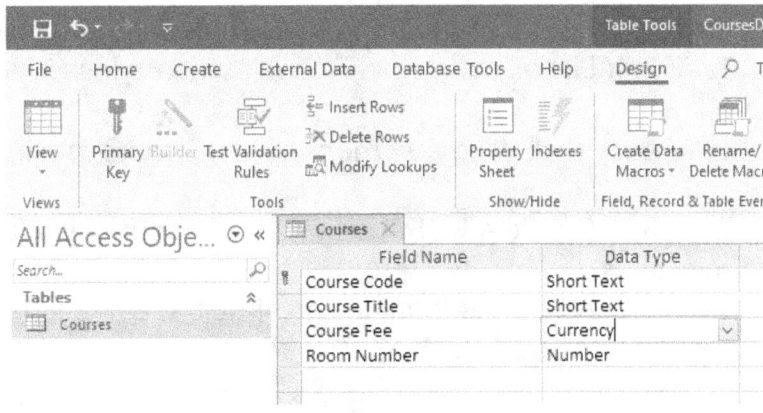

When the database structure is successfully created and saved, you will be presented with the database **control panel** where you should enter accordingly the Course details as shown below:

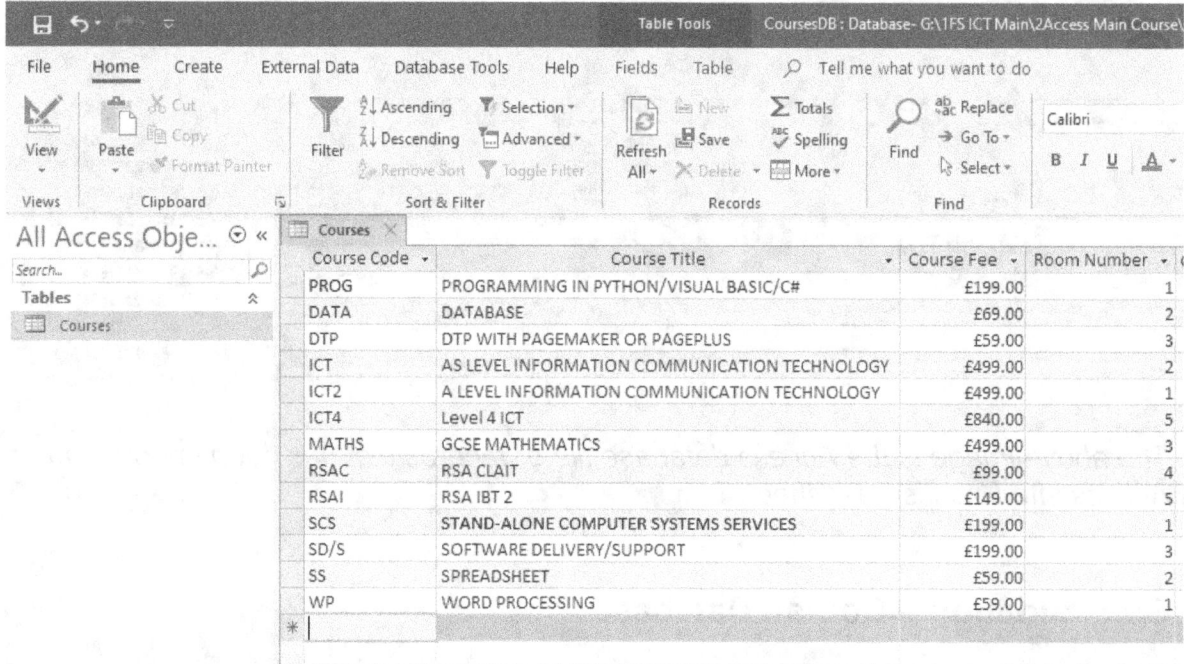

Manipulate the Database

- **Task 1:** *To manipulate the database, perform the following tasks:*
  - **Task 1.1:** Change the Field, **Course Fee** from **Number** to **Currency** (if not already done)
  - **Task 1.2:** Take a **screenshot** and **paste** in your evidence document
  - **Task 1.3:** Return to **Datasheet view**
  - **Task 1.4:** **Format** the Database to show fully all **Field headings**

- **Task 2:** *(for each task, take a **screenshot** and **paste** in your evidence document)*
  - **Task 2.1:** **Sort** the database in **ascending order** of Course fee
  - **Task 2.2:** List the courses with the Course code **ICT** – what room number is the course in?
  - **Task 2.3:** List all courses whose Course code starts with **IC**
  - **Task 2.4:** List all courses in Room **1** that are less than **£300**

- **Task 3:** *(for each task, take a **screenshot** and **paste** in your evidence document)*
  - **Task 3.1:** Create a **FORM** on the Course database (use default selections)
  - **Task 3.2:** Adjust the form design structure and alignments as aesthetic as you wish.

- **Task 4:** *(for each task, take a **screenshot** and **paste** in your evidence document)*
  - ○ **Task 4.1:** Create a **REPORT** on the Course database (use default selections)
  - ○ **Task 4.2:** Adjust the spacing and width of the field headings if any of the headings is truncated; ensure all records are visible in each column
  - ○ **Task 4.3:** Preview the Report
  - ○ **Task 4.4:** Take a **screenshot** and **paste** in your evidence document.

WORD PROCESSING APPLICATION SOFTWARE
Word Processing & Mail Merge Function

The Scenario

The academic performance of pupils in various course modules has lately been recorded in a straightforward database by Basildon Academy. The Academy wants to let the students know about their accomplishments by sending interim reports to their residences.

You have been charged with creating the mail merge document in your capacity as an IT support. Microsoft Windows and the Microsoft Office Suite serve as the foundation for the Academy's computer system.

Learning Outcomes:

i. How to use Word's Mail Merge functions to combine and import data from a source file outside of Word's application for processing business documents.
ii. Start a new Word document or open one that has already been written.
iii. Using merging fields as "placeholders," enter data, add to and update a letter or report.
iv. Format the letter or document accurately with no grammatical errors.
v. Identify the location on your computer where the recipient data list is kept.
vi. Select recipients and start the mail merge.
vii. Insert Merge Fields, Preview Merged Results, Finish and Merge, Edit Merged Document, Select All or Select a Specific Number of Merged Documents
viii. capture data screenshots, then put them in the evidence document files.

Introduction

Assumption:
This Word tutorial will presume that you have some experience with word processing and are probably familiar with Excel spreadsheets and/or Access databases.

Mail Merge in Word

Mail merge is an automated procedure for combining Form letters or other types of documents that are written in Word with a known list of recipients and/or "merge fields" so that the receiver sees the word document as if they had typed directly into it at the time of production. The automatic mail merging is made possible by placing specially created and generated "merge fields" on the Forms Letter or document. Four popular techniques can be used to create mail-merged documents:

1. Mail combine the recipients from an Excel spreadsheet into a Word document.
2. Mail merge a recipient list from Notepad into a Word document.
3. Mail combine a recipient list from an Access database into a Word document.
4. Mail merge a Word document to a recipient list that has been created inside a Word table.

To better demonstrate the act of importing and exporting data for this endeavour, mail merge from an Access database recipient list will be used. The relevant document can either be completed onto a pre-prepared document or created on-the-fly during the mail merging process.

To Merge Access database recipient list to Word

Open the Word document or Form letter where the mail merge fields need to be included (or create a blank Word document from scratch if you do not already have the document prepared). In this illustration, I'll open an Interim Progress Report document that has previously been prepared and add the necessary merging fields to it.

Process Steps:

1. Click on the Mailings menu bar to display the mail merging ribbon icons for this task.
2. To view the various document types that can be utilised with mail merge, select Start Mail Merge in the Start Mail Merge group;
3. After the Interim Progress Report document has already been opened, choose Letter from the drop-down list.

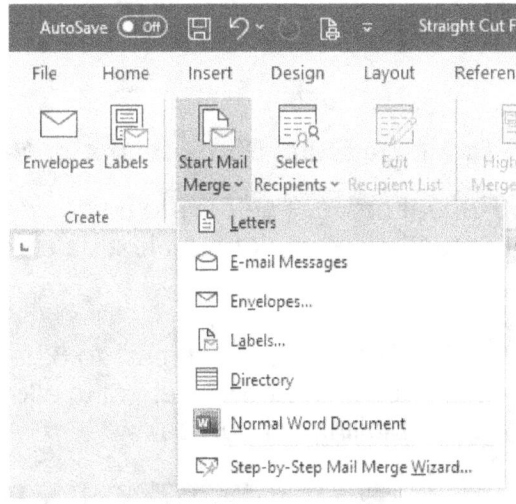

4. after that, select Use Existing List recipient type from the drop-down list by clicking on the next icon, Select Recipients;
5. As seen below, a dialogue box labelled "Select Data Source" or "Import Data" should appear:

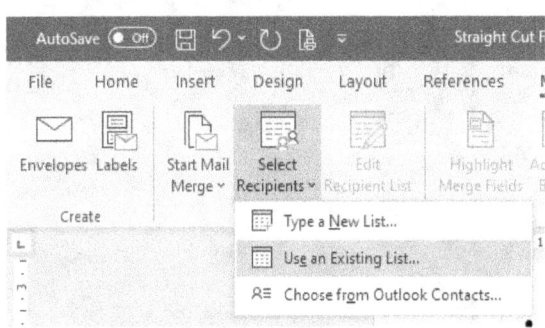

6. Next, navigate through your computer to locate the stored Access database file list (e.g. StudentDB), then click **Import**;

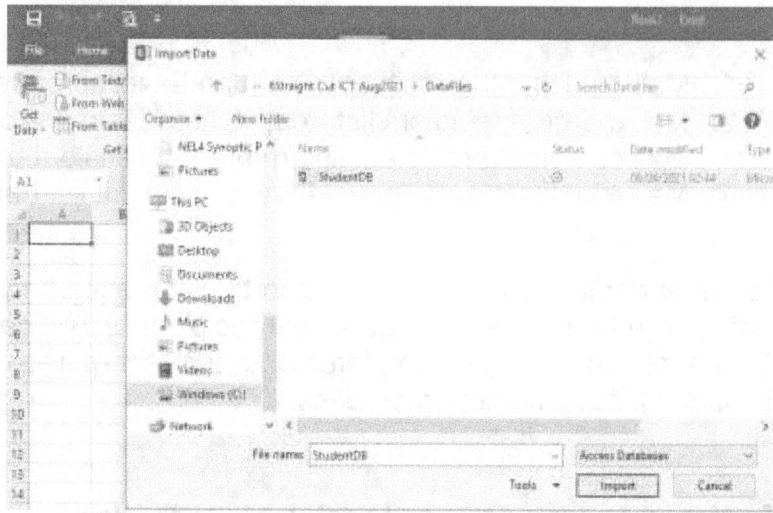

7. a dialogue box appears containing a list of recipient files;
8. select the student database file required then click OK.

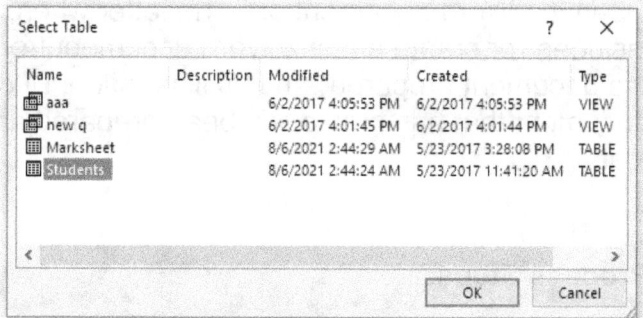

To Merge Excel Spreadsheet or Notepad Recipient list to Word

Repeat process steps 1 to 8 should you wish to merge Word document with an Excel Spreadsheet or Notepad text data.

9. Once process steps 1 to 8 has been completed, notice that all the ribbon icons are now enabled to allow you complete the mail merge process – see Mailings ribbon below:

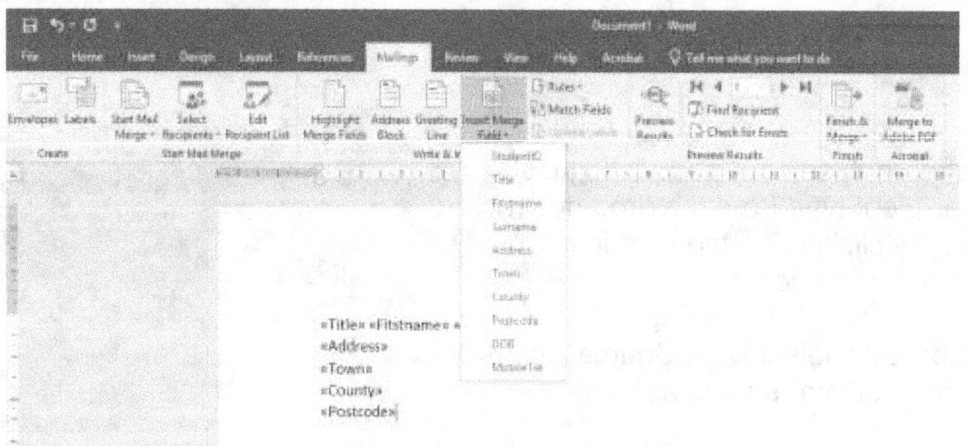

10. Now, on the Word document (form letter) containing the Interim Progress Report, position the cursor where you want to place a 'merge field', then click

the tiny picklist on the icon, **Insert Merge Fields** to reveal a drop-down list containing the available students' merge fields;

11. Select the required 'merge fields' for that cursor position remembering to put a **space** between fields on the same line
12. **Repeat** this process from within the **Insert Merge Fields** drop down list until all needed fields have been position correctly on the word document
13. See the **Interim Progress Report** document below and spot the various merge fields used. **Note:** this report document with the merged fields visible is referred to as **Unmerged document**:

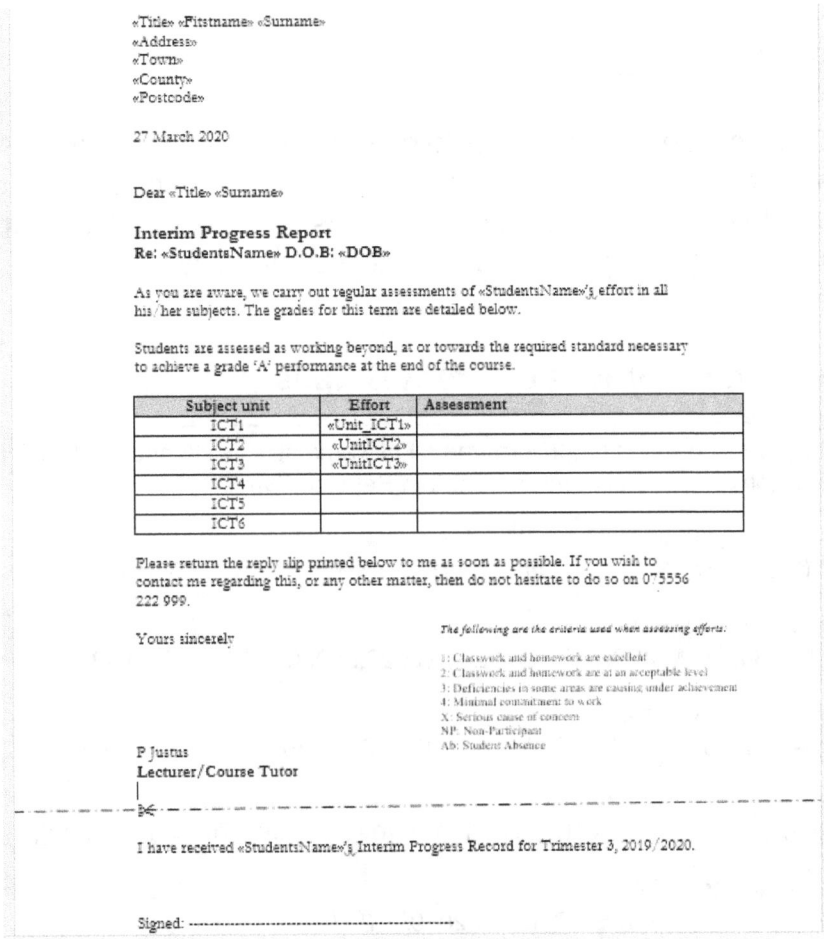

14. After you have spotted the merge fields, click on the **View Results** icon of the **mailings** ribbon menu bar to see the **results** of your mail merge and compare it with the unmerged document.
15. **Finish** the mail merge processes by clicking on the tiny picklist on the **Finish & Merge** icon of the **mailings** ribbon menu bar
16. You now have a choice of merging the documents straight to a printer, Send by Email Messages or merge to new individual documents - to be edited, saved or used as intended.

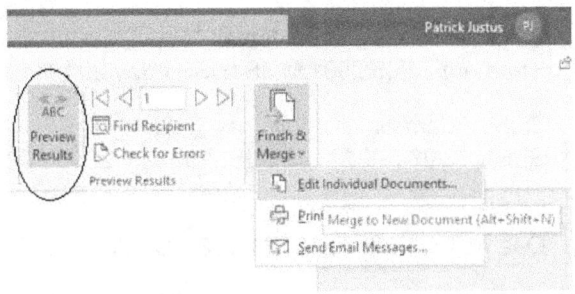

17. To merge into a new document and print, say, 3 pages of the reports only, click **Edit Individual Documents**... as indicated and select the necessary number of pages (from 1 to 3). To finish, press OK. Please take note that the completed report is referred to as a **Merged document**.

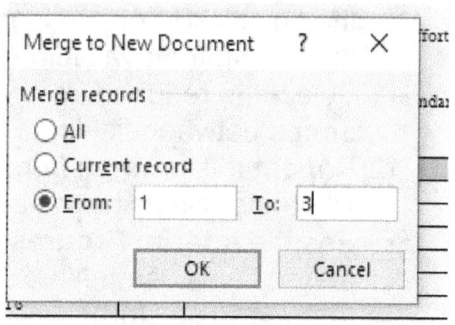

18. Take screenshots of the merged and unmerged documents and paste on your evidence document as required.

Consolidation – Mail Merge

You must create an enrolment letter to be sent to the student's parents in order to put your mail merge knowledge into practise. The information regarding the student-parent and a template of the enrolment letter is provided below. For the student-parent list, try using Notepad, Excel, or Access database.

Mail Recipients - Student-Parent Details

stStudentID,prTitle,prFirstname,prSurname,stFullName,stDOB,stGender,stClassID,stClassEn,
stHouse,SessionYear,FeeAmount,AmountPaid,Balance,PymtDueDate,

1,Mr,Musa,Farouq,Jubril
Farouq,23/05/2001,M,JS1,JSS1,Canary,2019/2020,58000,58000,0,01/03/2020

3,Ms,Franca,Matthews,Patrick
Matthews,12/08/2002,M,JS2,JSS2,Jay,2019/2020,58000,58000,0,01/03/2020

4,Miss,Rosemary,Hennessy,Rosemary
Hennessy,04/01/2001,M,JS1,JSS1,Mealy,2019/2020,58000,30000,28000,01/03/2020

20,Mrs,Raheel,Begum,Rashna
Begum,09/09/2001,F,JS1,JSS1,Mealy,2019/2020,58000,48000,10000,01/03/2020

21,Mrs,Nadia,Ahmed,Talatu
Ahmed,07/07/2001,F,JS1,JSS1,Cardinal,2019/2020,58000,58000,0,01/03/2020

22,Mr,Pirashath,Begum,Rohan
Begum,30/04/2000,M,JS3,JSS3,Canary,2019/2020,58000,58000,0,01/03/2020

23,Miss,Patricia,Thomas,Kelly Thomas,06/09/2000,F,JS3,JSS3,Jay, 2019/2020,
58000,58000,0,01/03/2020

24,Mr,Yasser,Khomeni,Ismail
Khomeni,20/06/2001,M,JS1,JSS1,Jay,2019/2020,58000,20000,38000,01/03/2020

25,Mr,Adam,Smith,John
Smith,12/03/2001,M,JS2,JSS2,Mealy,2019/2020,58000,40000,18000,01/03/2020

26,Mr,Arfan,Osama,Osman
Osama,04/12/2001,M,JS1,JSS1,Cardinal,2019/2020,58000,58000,0,01/03/2020

The Template Enrolment Letter:

METROPOLITAN INTERNATIONAL ACADEMY
Knowledge, Power & Eloquence

2 Miller Avenue
By Cecilia Junction
Off Iwofe Road
Port Harcourt, Nigeria
Email: info@mcbit.org

Date

ENROLMENT [SessionYear]

Parent Title: [prTitle]
Parent Firstname: [prFirstname]
Parent Surname: [prSurname]]

Student ID No: [stStudentID]
Date of Birth: [stDOB]
Gender: [stGender]

House: [stHouse]
Class ID Level: [stClassID]
Class Enrolled: [stClassEn]

Dear [PrTitle] [PrSurname]

Regarding the aforementioned, I am pleased to provide the enrolment and payment advice for the academic year [SessionYear] for [stFullName].

Please pay close attention to the outstanding amount (if any) that must be paid by the [PymtDueDate] in order to keep from being unable to attend the Academy.

I would like to express Metropolitan International Academy's profound gratitude for being chosen to start an early learning opportunity for your child or ward. We hope they have a successful and enjoyable stay here.

Yours sincerely
Vice Principal (Academic)

Fee Amount (N): [Fee Amount
Amount Paid (N): [Amount Paid]
Balance to pay (N): [Balance]

Underpinning Knowledge Questions

1. What does it mean when something is described as being in the "public domain"?
2. Identify two devices that have both input and output capabilities.
3. Describe one system modification that can be implemented to assist those with vision impairments.
4. Describe one reason why you shouldn't keep private or sensitive information on a memory stick.
5. Describe a scenario in which the system configuration View Network Status and Tasks might be applied.
6. Explain a technique to lower the possibility of data loss as a result of computer virus harm
7. Describe two cybersecurity best practices